# God's Revealed Plan For Man

## The mystery made known

Rudi Louw

The Holy Scriptures are just that; HOLY.

Statements enclosed in brackets were inserted into Scripture quotations to add emphasis or to clarify the meaning or truth of what is being said in those scriptures. *The integrity of God's Word to man was not compromised in any way. Due care and diligence was cautiously exercised to keep the Word of Truth intact.*

For example: The apostle Paul said in his second letter to Timothy in chapter three verse sixteen that:

*"All Scripture is given by inspiration of God* (literally God breathed), *and is profitable for doctrine, for reproof, for correction, for instruction **in righteousness**."*

# Content

The marvel of the Holy Bible ..............5

Acknowledgement .........................11

Foreword ....................................13

1. God's strategy ...............................19

2. A Manifestation of God's Glory ......43

Prayer .........................................49

3. *Your* attitude *is* important ...........53

4. The unction to function ..................71

5. The zeal *of* God ........................87

6. The glory of the Lord .................97

7. Making an impact ........................103

8. Missing out on God's plan ..........111

9. Consider the real glory ................135

10. Crowned with glory & honor ......151

11. Taking up arms .........................195

*12. You already qualify* .....................*219*

*About The Author* ........................*253*

# The marvel of the Holy Bible

## 1. The *theme* and *inspired thought* of Scripture continues *uninterrupted*.

It took *1,500 years* to compile the Holy Bible, involving *more than 40 different authors*, <u>yet</u> the theme and inspired thought of Scripture continues *uninterrupted*, from author to author, from beginning till end.

## 2. Absence *of mythical stories:*

Compare philosophies and theories about creation in the Middle East, Europe, Asia, Africa and Latin America, and you'll find mythical scenarios, gods feuding and cutting up other gods to form the heavens and the earth. In ancient Greek mythology, the Greeks see Atlas carrying the earth on his shoulders. In India, Hindus believe 8 elephants carry the earth on their backs.

But in contrast, Job, the oldest book in the Holy Bible, declares that *God suspends the earth 'on nothing.'* (Job 26:7)

***This was said millennia before Isaac Newton discovered the invisible laws of gravity that delicately balance every planet and sun in its individual circuit.***

In contrast to every other ancient attempt to give a creation account, *the Holy Bible pictures the creation of the earth in a very scientific manner.*

In Gen 1 for instance, the continents are lifted from the seas, then vegetation is created and later, animal life, all reproducing *'according to its own kind,'* ***thus recognising the fixed genetic laws.***

Finally we have the creation of man and woman, *all done by God in a dignified and proper manner, without mythological adornments.*

*The rest of the Holy Bible follows suite.*

*The narratives are **true historical documents**, faithfully reflecting society and culture, **as history and archaeology would discover them thousands of years later. Not only is the Holy Bible historically accurate, it is also reliable when it deals with scientific subjects.***

It was not written as a textbook on history, science, mathematics or medicine, *yet, when its writers touch on these subjects, they often state facts that scientific advancement would not reveal or even consider until thousands of years later.*

While many have doubted the accuracy of the Holy Bible, time and continued research have consistently demonstrated that the Word of God is better informed than its critics.

## 3. The Holy Bible is *intact*.

*Of all the ancient works of substantial size, the Holy Bible against all odds and expectations survives intact.*

**Compared with other ancient writings, the Holy Bible has more manuscripts as evidence to support it than any ten pieces of classical literature combined!**

The plays of William Shakespeare, for instance, were written about four hundred years ago, and written after the invention of the printing press.
Many of his original words have been lost in numerous sections, *yet the Holy Bible's uncanny preservation has weathered thousands of years of wars, contradictions, persecutions, fires and invasions.*

*Jewish scribes, **like no other manuscript has ever been preserved**, preserved the Holy Bible's Old Covenant text through centuries. **They kept tabs on every letter, syllable, word and paragraph**.*

*They continued from generation to generation to appoint and train special classes of men within their culture **whose sole duty it was to preserve and transmit these documents <u>with perfect accuracy and fidelity</u>**.*

Who ever bothered to count the letters, syllables, or words of Plato, Aristotle or Seneca for that matter?

**When it comes to the New Testament,** the actual number of preserved manuscripts is so great that it becomes overwhelming.

*There are more than 5,680 Greek manuscripts, more than 10,000 Latin Vulgate and at least 9,300 other versions; there exist a further 25,000 manuscript copies of portions of the New Testament.*

**No other document of antiquity even begins to approach such numbers.** The closest in comparison is Homer's <u>Iliad</u> with only 643 manuscripts. The first complete work of Homer only dates back to the 13<sup>th</sup> century.

# 4. In dealing with time, the Holy Bible *accurately foretells what will happen ahead of time, with unmatched results*.

**No other ancient work even begins to attempt this.**

**Other books claim divine inspiration, such as the Koran, the Book of Mormon, and parts of the Veda. *But none of these books contains predictive foretelling.***

**This one fact we know for certain, and it is undeniable: *While microscopic scrutiny would show up the imperfections, blemishes and defects of any work of man, it magnifies the beauties and perfection of God, just as every flower displays in accurate detail, the reflection and perfection of beauty, so does the Word of Truth when it is scrutinized*.**

Historian, Philip Schaff wrote:

*'…Without money and weapons, Jesus the Christ conquered more millions, than Alexander, Caesar, Mohammed and Napoleon. Without science and learning, He (Jesus the Christ) shed more light on things human and divine than all philosophers and scholars combined. Without the eloquence of schools, He (Jesus the Christ) spoke such words of life*

*as was never spoken before or since and produced effects, which lie beyond the reach of orator or poet. Without writing a single line, He (Jesus the Christ) set more pens in motion, and furnished themes for more sermons, orations, discussions, learned volumes, works of art, and songs of praise,* **than the whole army of great men of ancient and modern times combined**.' (The person of Christ, p33. 1913)

**Today, there are literally billions of Bibles in more than 2,000 languages,** *isn't it about time you find out what it really has to say?*

**Hey listen, the Holy Bible is all about Jesus, the Messiah, the Christ** *...and everything about Jesus Christ is really about YOU!!*

# Study tips:

**Read 2 Corinthians 5:14, 16, 18, 19, and 21.** In the light of these scriptures it should be obvious that if you want to study the Holy Bible *you should study it in the light of mankind's Redemption!*

*Daily feed on Redemption Realities,* especially Romans 1 through 8, Ephesians, Colossians, Galatians, 1 Peter 1, 2 Peter 1, James 1, 1 and 2 Corinthians, and the book of Acts.

# Acknowledgment

I want to acknowledge and thank one of my mentors in the faith, Francois du Toit, for blessing and impacting my life with revelation knowledge into *The Word of Truth.*

The portion on *"The marvel of the Holy Bible"* was borrowed from his website: http://www.mirrorword.net/ as students so often feel they have a right to do with things that come from teachers they respect. Just as Galatians 6:6 says: *"Let him who is taught the Word **share in all good things** with him who teaches."*

To all our other many dear friends and family, *and to all those who helped me with this project,*

*…but especially to my sweet wife Carmen:*

For all your love and support,

THANK YOU!

# Foreword

Thank you for taking the time to read this book.

Let me start off by saying that I am totally addicted to my Daddy's love for me; I am in love with Jesus Christ, *and that is enough for me!*

The love of God is so much more than a doctrine, a philosophy, or a theory; it is so much more and goes so much deeper than knowledge; it way surpasses knowledge, *we are talking heart language here,*

…therefore this book was not written to impress intellectuals with knowledge and philosophy, theologians with theories and doctrine, nor English majors with grammar and spelling for that matter,

*…so if you come up with any other definitions or find any language inaccuracies please don't use it to disqualify Love's own message I bring to you in this book.*

I write *to impact people's hearts;*

…to make them see the mysteries that has been hidden in Father God's heart, concerning Christ Jesus, and really *concerning THEM,* so as to arrest their conscience with it, that I may introduce them to their original design, and to their true selves; and *present them to themselves perfect in Christ Jesus* and *set them apart unto Him in love,* as a chaste virgin,

*"...for by Him all things were created... All things were created through Him and for Him. And He is before all things* (He has been in existence from the beginning, He has always been in existence and holds the place of preeminence over everything; He is the Prince of LIFE Himself), *and in Him all things consist"* (everything in creation is still working according to its design and is held together in Him; in His power proceeding from His heart of love. Everything and everyone finds their place of existence; their function and purpose; their place of significance; their very reason for being; their very home and belonging, in Him who loves them and gave Himself to them) - Colossians 1:16 & 17

**We are involved with the biggest romance of the ages;**

...therefore this book cannot be read as you would a novel; casually. It is not a cleverly devised little myth or fable.

**It contains revelation and *truth* into some things you may or may not have considered before. It is not blasphemy or error though.**

*It is the TRUTH of God, ultimate TRUTH, and therefore has direct bearing upon YOUR life,*

*…*the Word and the Spirit is my witness *to the reality of these things!*

Be like the people of Berea the apostle Paul ministered to in Acts 17:11. Open yourself up to study the revelation contained in this book, but be forewarned, do not become guilty of the sins of the Pharisees, **or you too will miss out on the depth of fulfillment God Himself, who is LOVE, wants to give you**.

(Jesus said of the Pharisees and Sadducees that they strain out every little gnat BUT swallow whole camels. What He meant by that is that *some people seem to have it all together when it comes to doctrine and they love to argue. It makes them feel important, but it is nothing other than EMPTY religious and intellectual pride. They know the Scriptures in and out, and YET they are still so IGNORANT about REAL TRUTH that is only found in LOVE; they are still so ignorant and indifferent towards the things that REALLY MATTERS.* They are always arguing over the use of every little jot and tittle and over the meaning and interpretation of every word of Scripture.

The exact thing they accuse everyone else of doing though; the precise thing they judge everyone else for, they are actually doing themselves, that is: they often completely misinterpret and twist what is being said, making a big deal of insignificant things, *while obscuring or weakening God's real truth; the truth of His LOVE.*

They are always majoring on minors, **because they do not understand the heart of God** and ***therefore they constantly miss the whole point of the message***.)

Paul himself said it so beautifully:

*"...the letter kills but **the Spirit BRINGS LIFE**;"*

*"...<u>knowledge puffs up</u>, but **LOVE EDIFIES**."*
I say again:

Allow yourself to get caught up in the revelation I am about to share. Open yourself up to study the insight contained in this book *not only with a desire to gain knowledge, but also **with anticipation** to hear from Father God yourself; **to encounter Him through His Word; and to embrace truth, in order to know and believe the LOVE God has for <u>you</u>, and to get so caught up in it, that you too may receive from Him; LOVES' impartation of LIFE.***

This revelation contains within it the voice and call of LOVE Himself to every human being on the face of this earth. If you take heed to it, it is custom designed and guaranteed to forever alter and enrich your life!

"Eye has not seen,
nor ear heard,
nor have entered
into the heart of man

the things
which God has prepared
for those who love Him.

But God has revealed them to us
through His Spirit.

For the spirit searches all things,
yes, the deep things of God.

17

Now we have received,

not the spirit of the world,

but the Spirit who is from God,

that we might know

the things that have been
freely given to us
by God."

1Corinthians 2:9 -12

# Chapter 1

## God's Strategy

When you read the title *"God's Revealed Plan for Man,"* you might be one of those skeptical people, who wonder whether there even is such a thing as *God's plan for man*,

…but the Bible declares and reveals that **God does indeed have a plan for our lives.**

Most of you who are not as cynical and skeptical as others, and who have taken some time to consider these things, probably already have an idea in your mind of what you think that plan might be.

Some of you might be thinking of God's individual plan for every individual person's life, like where he or she works, lives and attend church gatherings.

Some of you might be thinking of the future fulfillment of prophecy and the end times.

Still others might be thinking of what God is about to do in and though His Church in this generation.

Then there are also those of you who might be thinking of church-growth and evangelism strategies, etc...

In a way this book is about all of the above, it is about **_God's master plan_** for every individual person's life,

...it is about what **_God desires to do through His people_** in this generation

...and it is about **_God's Church-growth strategy_**,

...and about **_God's strategy for evangelism;_**

...**_BUT mostly it is about God's plan to love us;_**

...**_and to show us where we REALLY COME FROM,_**

...**_who we REALLY ARE,_**

...**_and where we TRULY BELONG!_**

You see I happen to believe that **_God's master Plan, His strategy,_** for our lives and for the Church and for this whole world **is all wrapped up in His LOVE.**

**It has everything to do with His _LOVE._**

**_Love's plan is so profoundly simple and beautiful and genuine and gentle,_**

*…and yet so genius in design that it is often overlooked!*

So, just what exactly is **God's Master Plan?**

…what is **God's Strategy** for our lives and for the Church and for this world?

I believe **God's Master Plan**, **God's strategy** for our lives and for the Church and for this world **IS THE SAME.**

**Yes, you read that correctly,**

**IT IS *THE SAME* plan and strategy**

**IT IS HIS WORD, period.**

(Sorry, FULL STOP, for all you British people out there, ha… ha… ha…)

*'What?'*

**I told you it was profoundly simple, didn't I.**

*'But… it can't be that simple Rudi, can it?'*

Friend, I know it comes as a shock and may sound somewhat unbelievable, **but don't you dare overlook the power of God's LOVE and the power of God's WORD!**

Don't overlook **HIS genius**!

1Corinthians 1:27

27 *"…God has chosen the foolish things to dumbfound the wise."*

Hebrews 11:3

3 *"…the worlds were framed **by the Word** of God."*

Hebrews 1:3 says:

3 *"…and upholding all things **by the Word** of His power…"*

God's genius is all wrapped up in **HIS** *Word!*

We cannot afford to overlook the power of **HIS** *WORD!*

I want you to notice I did not say:

We cannot afford to overlook the power of *the Scriptures…*

I said:

We cannot afford to overlook the power of ***HIS WORD!***

Sometimes in our minds, because that is what religion has taught us, **God's WORD** and the Scriptures is the same thing!

Now don't get me wrong, the *Holy Scriptures are inspired by the Spirit of God and of Christ,*

…who moved on men of old to write down their experiences, visions and words from God, *all for our benefit!*

*"…for doctrine (truth teaching), reproof, correction and instruction in **the word of righteousness**"* 2Timothy 3:16

Thus you see, *all the Scriptures prophetically point to one thing, '**righteousness**', and to **one person,***

…***that person is the Word of God made flesh,***

…*that person is the Messiah, Jesus, the Christ,*

…*who came to restore mankind, **us**, **back to righteousness!***

*The Scriptures **merely testify** of Him!*

Hebrews 1 makes it clear that,

*"God who at various times and in various ways…"*

(…in fragments of thought; in vague pictures; and incomplete revelation; in unclear prophetic messages; in mysteries written down and compiled as the Old Covenant Scriptures…)

"…God (in this way) *spoke to our forefathers in times past,*"

"(**BUT** He) has **in these last days** (at the end of time, [in the culmination of time] in the fullness of time) **spoken to us _in_ the Son**"

Another translation says:

"…**He has spoken SON to us**…"

This Jesus, **in His very person, and in His work of redemption, *is THE WORD of God*;**

"…**the crescendo of God's conversation with man!**" That's how the Mirror Bible puts it.

**He didn't just come with a message,**

…**He _is_ THE message!**

He didn't just come to give us a bunch of words; *some of them confusing and unrelated even,*

…no, **He _is_ THE WORD of God**, *singular, the totality and completeness of God's '**LOGOS**'*

**God has but one message,**

…and **Jesus _is_ that message!**

**So in the very same way then also, *the Scriptures is not 'The Gospel,'***

…**the gospel message is recorded in the Scripture,** *but the Scriptures in and of itself **is not THE GOSPEL**.*

Now don't get me wrong, please, I'm not trying to diminish the Scriptures in your eyes,

…and I am not trying to say that it no longer holds a place of real significance in my own life either, **it does.**

*I absolutely love the Scriptures and read it all the time.*

*I read and study many different translations **and have always seen it as vital to my fellowship and relationship with God.***

**If it weren't for the Scriptures, *none of us would even know what the gospel message is.***

**I dare say that most of us would not even know how to have a relationship with Father God if *it were not for the light of truth we heard about and found in the Scriptures.***

So the Scriptures *will never loose their place of importance in our lives,*

…*but the Scriptures **merely contain** the gospel message,*

…in fact, without understanding that gospel message, which becomes **the key to interpreting the whole Bible,**

…without that **key** of the gospel, *the Bible becomes a dangerous book that can leave you even more confused than you already are, because you would not know how to read and interpret it accurately in light of the gospel.*

Wars have been started over the interpretation of Scripture, and people **who have misunderstood** *its real message* have committed atrocities in the name of God, *supposedly inspired by the Scriptures.*

*It is absolutely imperative that we understand* **the message** *of the Bible and do not turn the Scriptures into something it is not!*

In the same way the Scriptures is not the *"Gospel,"* **but merely contain the gospel message,** in that same way, you also need to know that even though the books between Matthew and Revelation *is commonly thought to be the "Gospel," it is not really the "Gospel" either,*

**…it mere testify and bear witness to the gospel message and its impact upon the hearts and lives of people!**

…and even though the books between Matthew and Revelation are commonly known and referred to as the *"The New Covenant"* or *"The New Testament;"*

*…these books* **merely testify to and bear witness of that Covenant.**

**The New Covenant is a legal, living agreement,**

**…a conversation; a relationship between the Father and the Son** *who Covenanted together,*

*…***to redeem us and undo the fall of Adam!**

I am saying all this, so you *would not fall into the* **sentimental** *trap* of beginning to make something of the Scriptures **which it was never meant to be, as far as God is concerned!**

*…for then you end up worshiping the Holy Scriptures, turning it into an idol,* **like so many have,**

…and you hold your Bible tight under your arm, so that everyone would see you read it and obey it and are a good Christian,

…and you even go around kissing it and insist on it being the "WORD OF GOD" *and that nothing can be added to it or taken away from it,*

*…and yet you do not even understand **its true message,***

*…and that there is a "before" portion,*

*…and an "after" portion,*

*…and that the "old portion," which only prophetically pointed to the "new portion," **has been fulfilled and done away with!***

I did not say: *'Stop reading the books between Genesis and Malachi,'*

I said that the *"old portion"* meaning *"The Old Covenant portion;" the Jewish customs and traditions handed down **to them** in the Law of Moses **has been fulfilled and done away with.***

Please hear me correctly, I am not trying to offend anyone, but in our **ignorant sentimental worship of the Old and New Covenant Scriptures and of the Bible in general,** *we end up becoming just like the Jews and the Pharisees and Sadducees of Jesus' day.*

They made such an idol out of the Law, and out of the Scriptures, and their whole religious system of sacrifices, and all the customs and traditions handed down to them by their forefathers,

...so much so that *when the Messiah, the Christ, finally came;*

...*the One about whom all those things were about;*

...*the One about whom all those things were only a prophetic picture of;*

...*the One to whom all those things pointed,*

...**they could not receive Him and make the switch** from the *"shadows"* **to the *"substance;"***

...from the *"old"* **to the *"new"***

**He came and did away with** the *"shadow;"* with the *"old,"*

...**by introducing the *"new;"***

...**the *"substance"*** of those shadows;

*He Himself was the fulfillment* of all those things!

**All of the Scriptures, the totality of Scripture *is about Jesus the Christ;***

...**the original, the authentic, begotten only of God, *blueprint Son,***

…and because He is the original, the authentic, the blueprint son, that Jesus Himself *is all about YOU;*

*…YOUR original design was placed on display in His life,*

*…and then redeemed in His death;*

…Jesus is all about YOUR reconciliation with Father God;

…YOUR fellowship with your TRUE Father *restored!*

*That's what Jesus and redemption was all about,*

…restoring the image and likeness of God in Man,

…restoring US back to our original glory,

…the very glory we lost in the garden!

You see, *we who live in the New Testament times,* **have to grasp these realities.**

**We have to understand these things** or we will fall into the same trap as the Jews of old that lived in Jesus' day.

*If we do not comprehend God's true Gospel,*

*…**God's complete and completed message,***

*…**the culmination and conclusion of God's message in Christ,***

*…**if we do not comprehend God's final all inclusive thought and conversation with us in Jesus Christ, in the LOGOS,***

…then we will turn the portion of Scripture between Matthew and Revelation, with the inclusion of a few Proverbs and the Psalms, and maybe some other key favorite passages from the writings of the prophets,

*…into yet another **Law of Moses**;*

*…into yet another **type and shadow**;*

*…into yet another type of **the same death trap**;*

*…yet another **legalistic religious system of do's and don'ts to obey!***

*…and we will call it "**Christianity**"*

*…**but it is not!***

**That is not true Christianity!**

**Christianity is not, do, do, DO!**

**Christianity is: done, done, DONE!**

31

You see the Law and religion *is all about do, do, do!*

**Religion turns everything into legalism, and do's and don'ts we have to obey.**

**Religion always *focuses* on *conduct*,**

*...but the very foundation of our faith; the focus of our faith is "__BELIEVE__" and "__UNDERSTAND__,"*

*...**the focus of our faith __is not__ CONDUCT!***

Our obedience, our conduct, **is the *fruit*, the outflow of what we __believe__ and __understand__.**

That is what forms ***the foundation*** of our obedience; ***it's our __believing__ and __understanding__!***

In Romans 16:25-26 Paul talked about us,

*"...**being established according to** (or by) **his gospel,** according to (or through) __the preaching of Jesus Christ__ as pertaining to the revelation of the mystery,*

*...which was kept secret in ages past, **but which __has now been made manifest__,***

*...and __has then also now been made known__ to all the nations,*

*...__for__ THE OBEDIENCE __OF__ FAITH."*

Notice, he didn't say that these things have been manifested, and are now being made known to all the nations, and to you, *to make us all obedient* **to** *the faith.*

No, he talks about *the obedience* **OF** *faith.*

You see, in the gospel, *the very faith* **of** *God,*

(...**what God believes** *about the origin and design of the human being; the original and true identity of mankind; of every individual person on this planet;*

...**what God believes** *about the incarnation of that design and identity in Jesus Christ,*

...**what God believes** *about the work of redemption on the cross to rescue mankind and restore our original design and identity,*

...**what God believes about <u>these things</u>;**)

**<u>THAT FAITH</u> is what is being made known in the gospel**

...to bring about a specific kind of obedience; *the obedience* **OF faith**

You see; our faith is the product of **His faith** *being made known to us.*

It is *from faith to faith* - Romans 1:16, 17

OUR FAITH *IS OUR OBEDIENCE.*

Our faith is *our comprehension and yielding to His faith,* **embracing it as truth**.

**That embracing sets us free *in our inner-man;***

***...it renews our minds and transforms our whole mindset,***

**...and therefore it sets us free *in our very conduct.***

Thus our conduct now **is *a by-product of faith***.

It is a *by-product* of **a renewed mind;**

*...a by-product* of **truth we have comprehended and embraced;**

*...a by-product* of **God's faith!**

So, in our study together, **I want us to focus in on *the importance of God's Word; God's Message in Jesus***

***...that Message, and that focus* in that Message, is His revealed *master plan;***

***...Obtaining and also maintaining that faith-focus in the Message we discover in Jesus,***

**...that is His *strategy* for our lives and for His Church and for the whole world.**

34

**I believe we have underestimated _the importance_ of _God's_ Word; God's _Message to us in Jesus_ in His plan for our lives as well as in His plan for His Church and for the whole world.**

In the book of Isaiah, by the mouth of the prophet, _God Himself says this about **the ability, and the energy, and the impact, and the power of HIS WORD upon the thoughts and the hearts of people:**_

Isaiah 55:10 & 11

10 _"For **as** the rain comes down, and the snow from heaven…"_

(…bridging the gap and canceling the distance between heaven and earth,)

_"…**as** the rain comes down, and the snow from heaven and do not return there, **but water** (saturate) **the earth, _and make it bring forth_** and bud, that it may give seed to the sower and bread for the eater,"_

11 _"**So shall MY WORD be** that goes forth from My mouth;"_

_"…**It shall not return to Me void, but it shall accomplish** what I please, **and _it shall prosper_ in the thing for which I sent it**."_

**I want you to know that when God devised a plan to win back this world to Himself He came up with *only one* strategy:**

**HE SENT HIS WORD**

*John agrees with this in the gospel of John.*

He starts off his writing with:

John 1:1,

*"...In the beginning was The Word (...the LOGOS)..."*

*("In the beginning ...in the ARCHE* ...in other words, it means *to be first in order, time, place or rank* ...**was** [that is the word **EIMI**, it speaks of a timeless existence]

...thus, *"In the beginning ...in the timeless eternal existence was THE WORD; (the LOGOS),*

*...that WORD, that LOGOS was and is to be first in order, time, place and rank,)*

*"...and The Word, the LOGOS,* (... **the thoughts, the intents and purposes and declarations of God, the very logic of God; the opinion; THE ETERNAL TRUTH <u>according to God</u>**)

*...that WORD, that LOGOS was with God..."*

36

*"…The WORD, the LOGOS was* [again, the word **EIMI** is used, speaking of a timeless eternal existence]

…**thus**, (God's logic, God's opinion, God's thoughts and intentions; His purposes and declarations, God's eternal truth) was eternally in timeless existence *with…*

[…or *PROS,* equal with; face to face with; one with] *God;"*

Can you see with me how that God and His Word are *one!*

*…totally connected,*

*…absolutely inseparable,*

*…One and the same!*

*The WORD, the LOGOS is the very essence of God's being, the core of who He is,*

*…His very thoughts and desires and plans!*

God's WORD; that LOGOS *proceeds from* His heart; from His bosom!

*"…And THE WORD; that LOGOS became flesh and dwelt among us* (and within us),*"*

*"…and we beheld His glory…"*

*"…we beheld His (DOKAO)…"*

37

(The word "DOKAO" comes from the root word DOXA **which is an estimation of value term**;

*...it speaks of the weight or substance or worth of something or someone.*

*...it has to do with the true value of a person.*

*...It has to do with an accurate opinion, a favorable opinion of a person.*

*...It is based on truth or true worth and value.*)

*"...we beheld His glory (His DOKAO or DOXA);"*

*"...we beheld* [His person, who He is, and the very weight of His opinion; the substance of His truth; His accurate estimation of Himself, but also of us, *our true value and worth*]

*"...we beheld ...the glory of the (MONOGENES)..."*

*"...we beheld ...the glory of that which is begotten only of God..."*

*"...the glory of* [**the authentic,** (the *glory of*) **the original blueprint offspring;** (the *glory of*) **the only authentic original;** (the *glory of*) **the blueprint SON;** (the *glory of*) **the SON, begotten only**] *of the Father,*

*...we beheld that glory,* [**the blueprint of both the Father, and the Father's offspring**]

*...full of grace AND TRUTH"*

**The FULLNESS of grace,**

*...the FULLNESS OF TRUTH!*

*...God's ETERNAL TIMELESS TRUTH!*

*...about GOD, and about US!*

*...it was manifested in Him; in JESUS!*

*...it became flesh!*

**"In Him was LIFE** *and the life* (*...that life that* was manifested through Him,

...that life He lived in other words because of that LIFE that was in Him)

*...that life was the light of men."*

- John 1:1, 4 & 14

*He in His person is the very light; the very enlightenment of every person!*

(*...In other words, "He is the enlightenment of every single person on earth;"*

...meaning, the truth concerning who they really are; their origin, where they come from, and what they were designed for in relation to God *was revealed in Him!*)

***God's* plan for man, *God's* strategy**, is for us to become **one with *His Word* (one with His LOGOS,)** *that was from the beginning,*

…**so that we may become one with God;**

…**relating to Him intimately in relationship as our origin;**

…**relating to Him intimately as our Father;**

…**as Daddy!**

Later on in John He talks about wanting **us to abide in *His Word,***

…and about wanting ***His Word* to abide in us,**

…and about wanting **us to abide in Him,**

…and about **Him wanting to abide in us Himself, personally!**

**You see, God wants *His Word* and His very being to become flesh in us,**

…**He wants to reveal** *that original glory in which we were made; His very own glory* **through our lives!**

...He wants to reveal His DOKAO; His DOXA, His opinion, His truth, His reality, His value, His worth, *the wealth of His very being* through us.

He wants our lives to <u>BE</u> *the expression of His image and likeness,*

*...the visible evidence of His indwelling person;*

*...the visible evidence of His purpose;*

*...that design that was from the beginning.*

That is ***His* strategy**, ***His* master Plan,** *and there is no other plan.*

He has no other strategy.

God has no plan B.

He has no other plan.

*His LOGOS revealed* is His strategy.

*His WORD comprehended and revealed* is his plan.

*His LOGOS* <u>IN US</u> is plan A, B and C and all the way to Z if you like.

He has no other plan.

Did you know that YOU might be the only *"Word of God"* someone will ever read?

He wants to reveal *His Word, His LOGOS; His TRUTH* though our lives;

*...through our very person!*

He wants to reveal *His very image and likeness* <u>through YOU;</u>

He wants to reveal *Himself* <u>through YOU;</u>

*...<u>through your life</u>!*

He wants His offspring; His children, *to <u>be</u> His children!*

*...to be revealed as <u>His</u> offspring;*

*...to be revealed as such, being just like Him!*

He wants His companions in life, you and me, to be exactly that, *to <u>be</u> His companions!*

*...He wants to reveal that genuine inseparable companionship between you and Him to the world!*

I want you to be able to really *know* this to be true ...*to believe it* ...to have it *SETTLED* <u>down in the depth of your heart</u>, and in your spirit, by the end of reading this book.

# Chapter 2

## *A Manifestation of God's Glory*

Let's read what the apostle Paul has to say about this,

...maybe when you read how he puts it, what I am trying to say will become even clearer to you:

2Corinthians 2:15-17

15 *"**For <u>we are</u> to God, the fragrance** (the influence) **of Christ,** among those who are being saved, and among those who are perishing."*

16 *"To the one, **we are the aroma** of death to death, and to the other, **the aroma** (the influence) of life to life..."*

(How did this happen, how did we become that aroma; that influence?)

17 *"**FOR** we are not, as so many, peddling* (deceitfully exploiting for some kind of personal gain; some kind of warped and twisted intention) ***<u>The Word of God</u>, but as of sincerity, but <u>as from God, we speak</u>** in the sight of God, in Christ."*

43

2Corinthians 3:2-3

2 *"**You are our epistle** (There is a genuine connection between you and the message,) written in our hearts (There is also a genuine connection between you and us, you have become our friends, and you are like family to us now, we have been totally influenced together by the same message. That Message, which is written upon our hearts and which we are passionate about, is now also written in your hearts, and you have now become passionate about it too; therefore, we are both witnesses **to the reality of these things**.)*

(Who we are, in our very person, because of that connection with God and one another and with TRUTH, because of the abiding Word, the LOGOS,

*…who we are, our true inner person is) **known and read by ALL men**,"*

3 *"**you are manifestly an epistle OF Christ***

(…**in other words, you are a letter, a manifestation of *The Word,* of *the LOGOS,* a manifestation of *Christ*),**

*…ministered by us, **written** not with ink but **by the Spirit of the living God**, not on tablets of stone but **on tablets** of flesh, that is, **of the heart**."*

2Corinthians 4:2

2 *"But we have renounced the hidden things of shame, not walking in craftiness* **nor handling The Word of God** *deceitfully,*

*…***but** (by an open statement of the truth) ***by manifestation of The Truth*** **(by manifestation of** *The Word,* **by manifestation** *of redemption* **and of** *Christ* we are) **commending ourselves** (not our old, ignorant and confused, ugly selves we used to be, *but the beautiful Christ-like selves we now are, the beautiful Christ-life we now live,* we commend **that**) *to* **every** *man's* (every single person's) **conscience in the sight of God.***"*

In this Scripture Paul was talking about the impact that his ministry of *The Word; Christ Himself through the gospel message* had upon the hearts and lives of these people.

As he and his co-workers ministered *The Word of God* to them, he says, *they brought it in sincerity,* **as from God***.*

They were speaking right out of the faith-relationship and genuine fellowship and friendship they had with God through an understanding of *His Word, His LOGOS; an understanding of the gospel*.

**They literally became to God** *the very fragrance of Christ* **to these people.**

They didn't water down or adulterate *"the Word of Life,"* by mixing it with all kinds of Man-made philosophies and ideas, or the religious thoughts and traditions of men, trying to impress people.

They didn't try and gain the acceptance of people by mixing *"the Word of Truth"* with what was culturally and politically and religiously acceptable and popular thinking in their day.

*Neither did they use it deceitfully to manipulate people **for the sake of personal gain.***

No!

**They <u>preached</u> and <u>lived</u> *the Truth of the Gospel***

**...and so they became the aroma (the very influence) of life to those *who saw and wanted that Christ-life,***

**...*to those who wanted to get saved from an insignificant, inferior life to that Christ-life***

**...and to the rest, even though it was neither their message nor their intent, they became the aroma of death,**

**...*through their lives and their message, without even trying to, they contrasted and amplified the futility, emptiness and stench of a life lived outside of Christ ...outside of its original design and beauty!***

46

As a result, some hardened their hearts, responding negatively, *counting themselves unworthy of this eternal life…*

*…*but those who responded positively *renounced the hidden things of shame and also became* **_manifestly_ an epistle** *of Christ themselves.*

They too began to **commend themselves to every man's conscience** in the sight of God **by an open manifestation of _The Truth_,**

*…***exhibiting and displaying the beauty of the Christ-life**

Paul said:

***"You are an epistle****… known and read by ALL men."*

# Prayer

Father God, as we consider in our study,

...that *"The earth **shall** be filled with **the knowledge of your glory**,"*

...that *"The glory of the Lord **shall** cover the earth,"*

*"...as the waters cover the sea..."*

I thank you that we are not just dealing with *some temporary, and weak, Man-made promise,*

...but we are dealing with *the unchanging promises of THE ALMIGHTY GOD!!*

*Hallelujah!*

Father I thank you that *Your **desire** to unveil Your glory **is every bit as eternal** as You are,*

...and that it is **of such a nature** *that **no amount** of the power of darkness can hinder You.

Thank you that darkness itself *is rendered powerless.*

Thank you that You cannot be hindered by darkness,

*…just as much as no amount of darkness can hinder the light!*

**I thank you Father that You cannot be intimidated by Man's resistance.**

**No harsh wilderness front or appearance or environment, *nor wilderness experience,* will ever be able to intimidate You**

***…or cancel the integrity of Your glory.***

I thank you that You are not intimidated *by any size drought in Man's heart,*

*…or any desert-like condition whatsoever,*

*For You have purposed in Your heart, and determined and settled within Yourself,* to visit the wilderness *personally,*

***…through Your Word;***

***…through Jesus Christ;***

***…through Your Good News;***

***…through the revealing of Your LOGOS,***

***…through Your TRUTH made known,***

*…You have decided to turn the dry and thirsty land **into a fruitful field, with springs of water everywhere.***

Father thank you that *by Your Spirit,*

**…through Your precious anointed WORD,**

*…You are well able,*

**…to gain <u>such</u> entrance into our hearts,**

*…that Your <u>glory</u>,*

**(…the visible evidence of Your purpose and design),**

**…<u>will</u>** *shine forth from our lives to **all** the nations…*

Amen

# Chapter 3

## <u>Your</u> attitude <u>is</u> important

Believe it or not, it is **<u>your</u> attitude towards the Scriptures and the truth they contain;**

*…***it is <u>your</u> attitude *towards the Word of God*** that either frustrates or promotes **His plan** for your life.

*<u>You</u> either limit God or give Him absolute freedom to work in and through you.*

This is precisely what Paul said to the Thessalonians;

1Thessalonians 2:13,

*"For this reason we also thank God without ceasing, because* **when you <u>received</u> the word of God** *which you heard from us,* **you <u>welcomed</u> it** *not as the word of men, but* **as** *it is in* **truth***, THE WORD* **OF <u>GOD</u>***,* **which also <u>effectively</u> works in you who <u>believe</u> it***."*

**So in other words, the word's effectiveness in working in us is measured by our attitude, our receptivity, *our believing it and embracing it* when we come face to face with that word.**

I want you to notice; these people *"received,"* they *"welcomed,"* they *"believed,"* *"the word of God"*

They saw it not merely as the word of men, but they saw it as the *"word of __God__"*

They saw it as *"truth"*

*And **__that's why it was now also so effectively working in them__**.*

**Did you know that the Spirit unction upon your life,**

**(...the power of the Spirit at work in and through your life),**

**...__is directly related__ to the *treasuring* of the word of God __in your heart__?**

Proverbs 4:20-23:

20*"My son, **__give attention__** to my words; **__incline__** your ear to my sayings."*

21 **"__Do not let them__** depart **from your eyes (from your focus; hold on to your insight into what is being said); __keep them__** *in the midst of **YOUR HEART**,"*

(...**Embrace it; Love it,** in other words.)

*This thing is **a love thing** not just a head thing, not just a mind thing!*

54

I can just imagine Jesus reading this same scripture passage in proverbs many times, but one day while He was still reading it, *it became more* than just king Solomon's words to one of his sons, *suddenly it became more than mere words, more than ink on a scroll,*

*…**more than black ink on paper***

*Jesus read it and heard the voice of His Father;* **instantly those words became very precious; it became love-words; it became words of instruction from the very heart of His Father to His.**

In His spirit He could hear His Father say:

*"My Son, **give attention** to **My** words; **incline your ear** to **My** sayings. **Do not let them depart** from your eyes*

**(Keep this perspective, keep this view on things, keep the truth I'm revealing to you, keep your focus upon these things, keep My words); *keep them* (in your bosom, as love-words,)***"

"**Keep them *in the midst of YOUR HEART*,** *for **they are LIFE** to those that **find** them and HEALTH* (My power in operation) *to **all** their flesh."*

"***Keep your heart,*** **(cherish my love for you in your heart, and guard and protect the environment of your heart,)**

*...**with all diligence**,*

*...**for out of it spring** the issues of **LIFE**"*

When it comes to **The Word of God effectively** working in us, **and bearing fruit** in our lives, the **life contained in it** can **only** be **found,** it can **only** be **experienced,** when we begin to **develop and maintain** the **right attitude** towards it; embracing it fully**.**

If we want to have **LIFE** issue forth, **springing forth** out of our hearts; *if we want to have the rivers of living water **gushing** from our innermost being* **we will need to develop the same attitude towards God's word as a broody hen has towards her nest of eggs.**

I spent my high school years in an agricultural and technical boarding school in the small town community of Sannieshof in South Africa.

Practical Agriculture was one of my classes.

We had to get up at 5:00am to go and milk the cows on the farm; winter and summer, rain or no rain... ah, those were the days!

Anyway, on this farm we had chickens. *A lot can be learned from chickens believe it or not.*

We must develop the same focus; the same *attitude* towards God's word *as a broody hen has towards her nest of eggs* if we ever want to have the rivers of living water gushing forth from our innermost being;

…if we ever want to have real LIFE springing forth, issuing forth, out of our lives!

You see that broody hen *knows* that there is *more* to those eggs than can be seen by just looking at the shells.

*She knows that, hidden in those shells is precious life.*

So, *because of that knowledge she cherishes within herself,* she maintains her focus and never wonders far from that nest of eggs.

Her whole focus is on those eggs.

If she didn't regard the life in those eggs *as precious,* if she didn't *love that life,* she would forget those eggs; they would become less significant to her; she would not constantly return to go and brood upon those eggs.

We need to have that same broody attitude towards the TRUTH and the LIFE and LOVE hidden in the Scriptures;

*…prepared and designed for us to enjoy,* and confirmed in so many other things around us FOR THOSE WHO LOVE HIM.

You see; that broody hen is very egg conscious; she never takes her mind off of those eggs, for she knows that if she does, if she loses her focus, if she loses her interest, if they become less significant, those eggs *will never bring forth the life they were intended to bring forth; they will never bring forth **the life hidden in them***.

The life in those eggs is dependent on that hen's focus, on that hen's broody attitude. The life in those eggs needs the hen's broody attitude to come forth.

*If she didn't brood on those eggs, they would remain lifeless.*

So to sum it up, there are two very important things revealed to us in this example I'm using:

1. We have to **value** and **treasure**; we have to **love** the TRUTH and the LIFE and LOVE hidden for us to find and enjoy. It is in *the Word of God, in the Gospel revealed* in the Scriptures, *in the Message of God revealed* in those nuggets of truth. *We have to **value** and **treasure** and **love** it,* as much, and more, than a broody hen treasures her eggs, and then,

2. We also have to **brood** on the truth; on the word of God; on God's love for us revealed there; *on the work of redemption;* that means we have to **fill our minds and hearts** with the word of God; i.e. *the Gospel; with the love of*

*God; with redemption realities,* meditate upon it, **it has to be focused upon**, it has to have **first place priority** in our lives. *It has to become our treasure!*

**Our hearts need to focus on the love of God for us.**

I mean we have to begin to dig **with desire** into the Scriptures; into the word of God; i.e. *the work of redemption; into the message of the gospel; into the love of God for us personally and our worth and value to Him, revealed there in the gospel, in that work of redemption,*

...like a treasure hunter would feverishly and fervently dig for gold and precious jewels.

Let me suggest to you that the lack of a desire, and a hunger, even the lack of an attitude of treasuring; the lack of such feverish digging for that which is precious *is the very fruit of you not living and experiencing the abundant life promised by Jesus.*

*It's the very fruit of you not feasting on the great love with which He loves you.*

**Just being a religious person, attending a church, or even claiming to be a real Christian, does not produce these things.**

***It is only knowing and believing the love He has for you that does!***

You see, knowledge alone; knowledge of any kind; religious knowledge included, *doesn't satisfy your heart.*

The mind eventually gets tired of knowledge and the soul gets board with it.

*You can't feed or feast your heart on 1+ 1 = 2. The greatest knowledge in the world* eventually bore you after you have exhausted the subject and know all there is to know about it.

But you see, *the heart never gets tired of 'I love you.'*

God's love language in the gospel *is what our hearts feast on.*

We know, AND HAVE BELIEVED the LOVE God has FOR US!!

That knowledge; that knowing; that believing; that embracing; that treasuring of THAT TRUTH; that faith-focus makes all the difference in the world; *it satisfies, at the deepest level, the hunger of our hearts.*

I repeat:

The heart never gets tired of *'I LOVE YOU!!'*

Jesus talked about how important *our receiving* and *embracing that life-giving seed; that life-giving Word* is in Mark chapter 4 when He told His disciples a parable about seed being

**sown, and likened it to the word of God being sown**.

He said that **if they did not understand this parable, then they wouldn't understand anything about how the Kingdom of God (that is within you) operates either**.

Mark 4:3-20.

I want you to notice:

Mark 4:14

14 *"The sower sows **The Word**"*

(Part of our problem today is that *the accurate word is not being sown.*

*…*We are receiving all kinds of mixed seed and all kinds of influences, from various different, and sometimes even competing and opposing sources,

*…**but it's not the accurate gospel!***

It's an inferior seed, which brings forth an inferior harvest!

Some things you embrace in your bosom, even suck the life right out of you and produce no fruit whatsoever, *nothing that can sustain you.*

I once opened a wild flower seed packet and sowed it, in anticipation waiting, and thinking I am about to have beautiful poppies and daisies and pretty little delicate flowers all over my flowerbed, *but instead, all that came up was weeds!* What a disappointment!)

He goes on to talk about *our receptivity* and *the OTHER things in our lives* **that compete with the Word and its rightful place** …**its place of** ***full embrace and prominence* and *belonging* in our heart.**

He says in verse 15,

15 *"And the ones* **who receive The Word** ***(just) like* seed sown by the wayside, are** *those who* **when they hear The Word***,"*

(…they hear it, but they don't hear it with the right attitude, *they either don't understand it or they hear it with a flippant attitude, not realizing its value and what a treasure it really is,* **and so they don't treasure it, and do not allow it to penetrate or find a home in their thoughts or their hearts at all***,*)

*"…then* **Satan immediately comes to take away The Word that was sown in their hearts***."*

16 *"And the ones* **who receive The Word** ***(just) like* seed sown on stony ground, are** *those who* **when they hear The Word***,"*

(…they hear it, *but they are not serious enough about it, or they harden their heart towards it and dismiss it,* **they too don't realize its true value, and consequently don't treasure it like they should, they don't value it enough**,)

*"...they **immediately** (initially) receive it with gladness"*

(**But** **they were not totally convinced or took the time to thoroughly search out the matter – their hearts did not become thoroughly engaged**)

17 '*they have no root* (no solid, stable, attachment) *in themselves, and so endure only for a time.*"

*"As soon as tribulation or persecution arises against The Word, they immediately stumble."*

(They immediately abandon the truth of the word and get caught up in their circumstances and in this natural life again, living their lives as mere men cut off from God.)

18 *"Now the ones* **who receive The Word (just) like** *seed sown among thorns, are those who* **when they hear The Word**,"

(*...they hear it, but they too don't treasure it enough, it's not important enough to them,* **they underestimate its value, and have too many other things they value, that compete for their attention and affection**,)

19 *"and they* **afterwards** <u>**allow the cares of**</u> <u>**this world, the deceitfulness of riches, and**</u> <u>**the desires for other things to enter in and**</u> <u>**choke The Word**</u>*,"*

(…these things stop the word from having its influence because instead of a passionate faith-focus in the love and truth of God being developed, an alternative focus is established in the cares of this world, in the deceitfulness of riches, or in desires for other things. These things neutralize the word; its message and power, it cancels out its effect; it slowly kills the word's faith-focus and passion,)

*"…***and,** (as a result) *<u>**they bear no fruit in**</u>* <u>***their lives***</u>*."*

(God's whole purpose with **the word of the** **gospel; the word of His love; the word of** **truth,** is first for the word to build a passionate faith-focus in you in order to bear fruit in you to sustain you, *and then for that word and that* *focus, and for you,* **to bear fruit in your life.**

Satan knows that the only way he can stop God's purpose from coming to pass is **to steal** *The Word* <u>**out of your** *heart*</u>.

**When we don't realize what we receive, or** **we don't receive** *The Word* **with** *the correct* **attitude**, **or** *don't treasure it like we should*, **with a passionate faith-focus, then we allow** **Satan to steal** *The Word* **and to frustrate** **God's purpose.**

***The Word* has to have the right environment or it will never bring forth fruit in your life.**)

20 *"But the ones **who receive The Word** like* __**seed sown in good soil**__**,** *are those who **when they hear The Word** __accept it__ **(receive it, embrace it, welcome it with open arms, believe it, value it, treasure it, understand accurately and fully, and love it's message) and (therefore) goes on to bear fruit:**

*…**some thirtyfold, some sixtyfold, and some a hundredfold**"*

Listen, *God has nothing less than a hundredfold purposed for us. Only our attitude, only our passionate faith-focus* determines whether it will be thirty, sixty or a hundredfold.

**If there is nothing wrong with the seed, it can only be the environment and the content of the soil that determines the quality and quantity of the fruit.**

That is why Jesus said in Mark 4:24

*"Take heed to what* (it has to be good seed) *you hear* (but also how you hear it, with what *attitude;* with what *receptivity;* with *what kind of embrace – a full passionate embrace – or a casual religious embrace – a weak and inferior embrace*).*"*

*"…**With the same measure you use, it will be measured back to you;***

*…and to you **who really hear**, (or who understand, and love, and passionately embrace, and hold on to and treasure what you hear) **more will be given**.*"

James 1:21 says:

"*…**receive** with meekness (without cynical suspicion, with openness, with no resistance and hardness of heart) the **IMPLANTED** word, which **is able to save your souls***"

"*…**save your souls**…*"

(He is not talking about going to Heaven one day, but about **your soul being rescued and getting satisfied and strengthened to now be able to stand against all the attacks of the enemy**;

…He is talking about your soul **being made totally whole through truth and LOVE, so that you don't have to give in to temptation anymore**.)

The word "*meekness*" means:

…**to humble yourself, to submit yourself willingly, to yield without resistance**

So in this Scripture that word "*meekness*" has to do with **the attitude of your heart**, especially towards God.

It means you are **receiving the word** <u>without disputing or resisting</u>.

In other words, you are **receiving the word without double-mindedness, trying to cling to your old opinions**.

That's what *"meekness"* means.

**Receiving the word** with *"Meekness"* means **you are willingly cooperating** with God.

It means **you are yielding to His word**, to its influence upon you, **to receive the full impact of His word**.

It means **you fully believe His word**.

It means **you are embracing the word fully and falling in love with it.**

**You are falling in love with what He is saying,** *so that you may fall in love with Him.*

*That is the only thing that will ever save your soul; rescue it, give it a home, a place of belonging, and make it whole!*

See, **falling in love is something you allow to happen to you,**

…**it is something that happens to you,** *it is not something you have to try and do,*

...there is no faking it,

...you don't have to fake falling in love,

*...either you embrace God's message as truth and fall in love with it and with Him, or you don't,*

*...but there is none of our own efforts involved!*

*It's either real, or it's not!*

*The message is either real or it's not!*

**If the message is authentic and real to you,** *then your falling in love with it is just the most natural response in the world!*

**If you listen long enough to the true gospel,** *until you fully understand it and grasp it, and begin to embrace it,*

*...you can't help falling in love and becoming addicted to it and wanting to hear more and dig even deeper, and treasure every nugget of its truth you discover.*

**It then begins to rescue your soul and guard and protect your soul from any other influence,**

**...and other inferior beliefs and knowledge that is full of subtle lies and deception,**

...and which eventually leads to emptiness and sin and destruction.

James 1:18 says:

*"Of His own will **He brought us forth <u>by the word of truth</u>**"*

So, it is **by revealing** *"His own will,"*

...**by revealing His own truth and desire of us to us;**

...**by revealing His own love for us to us,**

...***it is by revealing these things to us,***

...**in** *"the word of truth;"* in the *"the gospel of our salvation;"* in the *"the gospel of our redemption,"*

...**it is by revealing these things** *and persuading us in them;*

...**it is by us believing it and falling in love with its message,**

...**that we are now being** *brought forth,*

...*revealed* **as His children,**

...**living out the life we were designed for**,

...**this abundant LIFE with God, this eternal LOVE LIFE;**

...we are being brought forth and revealed as God's children by this source;

...by this gospel truth;

...by this *love and empowerment* we find in *His Word.*

# Chapter 4

## The unction to function

In Acts 20:32,

*"**The Word of Truth**"* is also called:

*"…**the Word of His Grace**."*

He goes on to say that this *"**Word of His Grace**,"*

*"…**is able to** **build you up** **and** **give you an inheritance**…"*

Psalms 2:8, God says,

*"Ask of Me, and I will **give you the nations for your inheritance** and the ends of the earth for your possession."*

*"**The Word of His Grace;**" "**The Word of Truth**," focuses on the work of grace*

(…**on the incarnation, on the life, death, burial, resurrection and ascension of the human race in Jesus Christ, *you included,***

…**because He fully represented us** in that work of redemption; that work of grace**.)

It is only understanding into that *"Word of Truth;"*

…fully understanding that *"Word of His Grace;"*

…**falling in love with that work of grace** that can…

*"…build you up and give you an inheritance."*

**It is only understanding into these things;**

…**believing it;**

…*falling in love with its message to you and to the whole world*

…**that gives you the *unction in your spirit* to aggressively lay a hold of your inheritance.**

**When insight into these things begins to lay a hold of your spirit** *you too will begin to quote the words of Isaiah over yourself, just like Jesus did.*

Luke 4:18 & 19

18 *"The Spirit of the Lord is upon ME, because* **He has anointed ME to preach the gospel** *to the poor (…the poor in spirit, whether they are naturally poor or not,*

…of course the gospel declares and reveals that there is deliverance from poverty to the naturally poor as well)."

*"He has sent **ME** to heal the brokenhearted,"*

*"...**to preach deliverance** to the captives"*

*"...**and recovery of sight** to the blind (both spiritually and literally blind),"*

*"He sent me ...**to set at liberty** those who are oppressed (by ignorance, sin, sickness and the forces of darkness; the forces of the devil),"*

19 *"He sent me ...**to preach the acceptable year of the Lord's favor"***

(Note: The events that took place, and became known as *the work of redemption,* **happened in the fullness of time; in the year of the Lord's favor**;

…that whole time period is known **as the acceptable year; or the year of the Lord,**

*...**and it refers to the Lord's favor being extended to all generations, even until now, even until the end of time!***)

Let's also read 1John 2:20 & 21,

20 *"But **YOU have** an anointing from the Holy One, and you (therefore) know (intimately,*

*accurately know and understand, have insight into) all things."*

21 *"I have not written to you because you do not know **The Truth**, <u>but because you know it</u>, and that no lie is of **The Truth**..."*

(In other words:

I have written to you because **you know The Truth; because you believe The Truth, and have fully embraced The Truth; and you have an anointing from the Holy One because of it, because of that Truth; because of that faith; and it is not a lie; <u>*that (faith) that TRUTH* is the anointing</u>**)

Verse 24 says

**"Therefore let that**... (Let the Word of Truth; the gospel; the work of redemption and reconciliation back to our original Father and our original design, let THAT) ...*abide in you*,"**

**"...*which you heard from the beginning.*"**

**"*If what you heard from the beginning*...**

**(The Word of Truth; the gospel message; the understanding of what was from the beginning and is now restored to us;**

**...if THAT truth) <u>*abides*</u> in you,"**

*"...**you also will abide in the Son and in the Father**,"*

And verse 27 continues,

*"But the anointing which you have received from Him abides in you, and you do not need that anyone teach you, but as **the same anointing teaches you** concerning all things, **and is Truth**, and is not a lie, (**In other words, Truth is the anointing**) and just as it has taught you, **you will abide in Him**."*

Jesus said in John 15:10

*"If you keep* (believe, value and treasure) *my commandments* (the things I commanded you to believe because they are true and worthy of all acceptance,

...in other words **if My Word; My gospel message; revelation into My work of redemption abides in you**)*,"*

*"...**you will abide in my love**, just as I also have kept* (believed, valued and treasured) *My Father's commandments* (the things He commanded me to believe because they were true and worthy of all acceptance,

...in other words **I allowed My Father's Word to abide in Me, and I understood the purpose of the cross, and therefore I went** through with it; with that gruesome work of redemption,

...I kept; believed; embraced; valued and treasured My Father's Word; His commandments) ...*and abide in His love.*"

Jesus <u>believed</u> His Father's Word, <u>lived</u> His Father's Word and <u>did</u> His Father's work;

He <u>embraced</u> The Spirit of Truth (The Spirit of God), speaking to Him through *The Word* and becoming the motivation in Him to do His Father's work.

Jesus was abiding *<u>in</u> His Father's love;* He was experiencing it; He was encountering it; He was enjoying a certain intimacy in relationship with His Father; He was having constant fellowship with His Father,

...*because He was abiding in His Father's Word and in His Spirit and in His LOVE*

If you want the presence of God; the experience of Him; intimacy with Him to increase *and come to fullness* in your live;

...if you want an increase in the anointing,

...then let *The Word* <u>abide</u> in you,

...and <u>*yield to*</u> *The Spirit of Truth* (the Spirit of God) *who speaks through The Word,*

…and believe *The Word*, live *The Word*,

…*do what the Spirit of Truth and Love inspire within you;*

…*give expression to the Father's working within you!*

If you yield to *the Spirit of Truth and LOVE,* the anointing will increase in your life.

Let me emphasize again:

Spirit unction, the anointing operating in your life, is directly related to you treasuring *The Word of Truth and Love* in your heart.

*The Word of TRUTH; the Word of HIS LOVE* and the anointing are inseparable.

The Holy Spirit isn't called *The Spirit of Truth* for nothing.

He is Love and proceeds from Love, and He represents and presents the TRUTH to our spirits.

That is why Paul said that,

*"Faith works by love"*

…and he told us to,

*"…speak the truth in love"*

**See; the truth is all wrapped up in the love of God.**

**There is no accurate truth outside of love!**

**The truth originated from Love Himself.**

**If you separate truth from love, all you are left with is legalism and doctrine, and there is no life in that.**

**The anointing;** *the life giving love and power of God* **is directly connected to the Word of Truth abiding in your heart!**

2 Peter 1:2 & 3

2 *"Grace* (everything God did in Christ on Man's behalf)

…*and peace* (the byproduct of grace;

…in other words everything we experience in God through faith in what that grace gave us;

…all of THAT) <u>*be multiplied* (gets multiplied)</u> *to you* **in the knowledge of Him**…*"*

(In other words, through **The Word,** through understanding of that Word, through faith in that Word…)

3 *"<u>His divine power</u>* **has given to us all things** *that pertain to life and godliness,"*

How?

*"…**through the knowledge** (through **The Word**) **of Him**…"*

*"…who called us **to enjoy His own glory and virtue**"*

Note: **God's divine power and the multiplication of it in our lives is directly linked to the knowledge of Him,**

*…***to** *"**The Word of His Grace**"*

You see experiences and encounters in God are great, and they can add a lot to our lives,

*…but they only enhance what **The Word** already says.*

**All experiences and encounters must rest on the foundation of *The Word* and be judged by *The Word*.**

*"But even if we, **or an angel from heaven*** (what a powerful experience), *preach to you **any other gospel than what we have** preach<u>ed</u> to you, let him be accursed."*
                                           -Galatians 1:8

*"Heaven and earth will pass away, **but <u>My words</u> will by no means pass away**."*
                                           -Matthew 24:35

*"For You have magnified **Your Word** above all Your name."* -Psalm 138:2

*"Man shall not live by bread alone, but **by every Word** (The authentic original, complete Word or LOGOS) that proceeds from the mouth of God."* -Matthew 4:4

**(I am not negating the fact that the Holy Spirit is a real person, that God and the Holy Spirit are one, and that He not only can, but also does actually speak to people.**

**When God speaks to you, it is the Holy Spirit that speaks to you. He often speaks to all those who have a relationship with God as Father.**

***The Holy Spirit does not just speak to us through The Scriptures.***

I too by the power of the Holy Spirit went through an immersion experience in the Holy Spirit at the age of 8 and cannot deny the reality of these things, these experiences in Him, nor can I deny the reality and the depth of the relationship I now have with Him,

...all I can tell you is that since that day I have come to know God the Holy Spirit more intimately *in person as the very Spirit of my Father, as the very Spirit of Love, as the very Spirit and person of Jesus, of God Himself.*

I had a wonderful encounter that day when I was immersed in the Holy Spirit.

That experience and encounter with God changed my life for the better and I have not been the same since.

It was equal to the experience of forgiveness and embrace I encountered when I first opened up to God's love and salvation, and embraced His acceptance of me, and it was every bit as powerful.

I can still remember when that immersion in the Holy Spirit happened to me. It was around 8:00pm one Tuesday night at a prayer meeting in the church my family attended.

I cannot imagine my life without that experience of immersion into Love Himself, or without His nearness, which has now become my daily portion.

If you have never been immersed in the wonderful Holy Spirit; immersed into Love Himself, just like I and all the believers in the book of Acts have experienced; *you sure are missing out on the most glorious thing you can ever experience in life.*

…it is more than an experience really; *it is the start of an ongoing daily encounter with God in the spirit!*

I am not negating these things, so please hear what I have been saying and what I am about to say correctly.)

In today's religious church world, pastors have tried everything to keep the churches motivated,

…but they do not seem to be able to break beyond a thirtyfold increase in their ministries.

So many of them have been deceived and deceiving their congregations into running after all kinds of experiences, and this, that, and the other thing,

…thinking that that might do it,

…that might just be the recipe that works.

They are blown about by every new wind of teaching,

…and every new wind of revival and refreshing that comes along in the body of Christ.

And although we all need and treasure fresh encounters in God's presence, these people running from one experience to another, **do not have enough substance; enough sustaining faith substance; enough truth substance from the word of truth; they do not have enough of the substance concerning the work of redemption;** *they do not fully understand for themselves their* *redemption and it's full implications in their lives,*

...and therefore they are unable to sustain a daily encounter, a daily sustained satisfying intimate fellowship and encounter with God!

There is a void, which remain in their spirit, which cannot be filled.

They have become like junkies needing the next fix all the time, *and yet they remain empty.*

While there is nothing wrong with gathering together in big meetings, or with having wonderful encounters and experiences in the presence of God,

...these people who do not have **the sustaining substance of** *The Word of Truth; i.e. their revealed value and worth and identity; the revealed love of God the Father for them personally* **abiding in their hearts and lives,** they keep going from one big meeting to another,

*...hoping to feel the anointing or to get more of the anointing to come into their lives,*

...when all they really need to do is to get *The Word of Truth; to get the revelation of their true worth and their true value and their true identity,*

*...all they need to do is to allow their Daddy's love to abide in them and to fulfill and sustain them in intimate friendship and fellowship with Him.*

They do not realize that their biggest need, more than anything else, is for *The Word of Truth, and the LOVE of their Father God for them personally, revealed there in the Word of Truth,*

*...for that LOVE and TRUTH to become a REALITY to them and within them!*

It is the very foundation of a deep daily sustained relationship and encounter with God!

I say again:

While encounters with God and experiences in His presence add so much to our lives,

*...our biggest need is for The Word of TRUTH and LOVE to be a REALITY to us,*

*...for it is the very thing that sustains those deep encounters of His love and that constant friendship and fellowship with Him!*

We need *God's Truth;*

...we need *the love of God;*

 ...we need the embrace of *The Word;*

 ...*that comes through the word!*

There is a deep sustained intimate encounter with God waiting for you in the Gospel;

...in His Word of Truth;

...in His love for you revealed,

...*that encounter will last beyond seasons.*

The *eternal presence* of God is in His *eternal Word.*

That Word was incarnated and glorified in flesh, so that in our *interaction with The Word and our understanding of what is revealed there,* we might have New Life in Him NOW!

...everlasting life!

*"The words I speak to you are Spirit and life!"* -John 6:36

*"Whoever drinks the water I give them shall never thirst again!"*

*"Indeed, the water that I will give them will become within them an artesian well, bubbling up within them constantly eternal life forever!"*                              -John 4:14

I believe *God's <u>Word</u>* is *<u>God's</u> strategy* to win you and me and this whole world over to Himself,

...and to bring us all into His presence, through an intimate faith-encounter *that will take us beyond seasons,*

...it will continue and last all the way into eternity.

**Hallelujah!**

I suggest to you today that *God's* strategy *has so much more potential* and will prove to be *so much more effective*

*...than all our motivational, self-help, and church-growth seminars <u>combined</u>.*

# *Chapter 5*

## *The zeal <u>of</u> God*

**Have you ever thought about the fact that there is a very big difference between having a sincere zeal <u>for</u> God and actually having <u>the zeal of God</u>?**

It never ceases to amaze me how easily people can develop *a misguided zeal,* **sincere, but misguided none the less.**

Paul the apostle, felt compassion for the Jews of his day; he could fully understand their passion *for they too had a zeal for God,* just like he once had.

He says: *"…they have a zeal for God…"* *"…**but not according to knowledge**"*
                                    - Romans 10:2

I don't know about you, but I would much rather have a zeal **according to knowledge,**

…I would much rather have, *the zeal of God;*

…*the love of Christ constraining me;*

…*the grace of God at work in me,*

*...**because of an accurate conclusion in the Gospel**,*

...than some misguided *zeal **for** God*

I believe it makes all the difference in the world.

I believe it means the difference between constantly falling short and actually living to our full potential;

...living out, or giving expression to, our original design.

The Gospel is what defines our lives.

I say again:

...the fullness of life is all about living out our full potential; *our true design*

...giving expression to *His fullness in us,*

...*"of His fullness have we all received, grace upon grace!"*

I believe the zeal *of* God;

...*an accurate revelation of the gospel;*

...*insight and understanding into the gospel;*

...an accurate conclusion in the gospel;

88

**…that deep fulfillment and love I constantly experience and live in because of it,**

*…will out produce a zeal <u>for</u> God any day!!!*

Paul said in 1Corinthians 15:10,

*"…<u>I labored</u>, (I bore fruit), <u>more abundantly</u> than them all, **yet not I, but <u>the grace of God working in me</u>**."*

He makes it even clearer in Colossians 1:28 when He said,

*"I also labor then… **<u>according to His working</u>**…"*

**(*…according to His truth; His influence; His energy; His motivation;***

*…His anointing and His love and passion)*

*"…which **<u>He so mightily inspires</u>** (awakens and kindles) within me…"*

**I believe that <u>the zeal of God</u> is <u>in HIS WORD</u>!**

**The growth of the early Church happened because of the impact of *The Word of Truth* upon their hearts.**

*Their conclusions, conviction, and encounter, in The Word of Truth, was the source of their zeal and anointing.*

**That is why they saw so many miracles and made so many disciples.**

Acts 14:3,

*"Therefore…* (**because of the impact of *The word of Truth* upon their hearts,** they were)

*…***speaking boldly** *in the Lord,*

*…who was* (*…*the Lord Himself was)

*…***bearing witness <u>to the word of His grace</u>,**

(*…***to the gospel of Love's intervention and redemption of the human race)**

*…***granting signs and wonders to be done by their hands***"*

Do you notice?

*"…***the Lord Himself… was bearing witness <u>to the word of His grace</u>, granting signs and wonders to be done by their hands***"*

Acts 6:7 says:

*"…and the word of the Lord* **kept on spreading***…"*

What word?

*"****The word of His grace;****"*

*"The word of TRUTH;"*

*"The word concerning the success of REDEMPTION"*

*"The word of His LOVE and how He came and RESCUED US"*

*"…and **the number of the disciples continued to increase greatly** in Jerusalem."*

In Acts 12:24 we read:

*"…but the word of the Lord…"*

(In other words; *"The word of His grace;"*

*"…the word of TRUTH;"*

*"…the word concerning the success of REDEMPTION"*

*"…the word of His LOVE and how He came and RESCUED THE HUMAN RACE," that word*)

*"…**continued to grow and to be multiplied**"*

Acts 19:20 says:

*"…the word of the Lord…"*

(He is still talking about *"That Word of His grace;" "That Word of TRUTH;" "That Word of His LOVE and REDEMPTION"*)

91

It was *"...**growing mightily and prevailed.**"*

How did this happen?

I mean what was the cause?

In Acts 4:20 the apostles reveal their secret:

*"...**for we cannot stop speaking** of what we have seen and heard."*

**(...what we have grasped and understood and believed ...that which captivated our hearts had our undivided attention and devotion ...we fully embraced it and focused upon it as God's Truth, and we, therefore, also *experienced its reality!***

**...It became the source of an unquenchable, undying, unstoppable zeal within us! We could not help but bare its fruit!)**

Jeremiah explains it like this:

*"...but if I say, I will not remember Him or speak anymore in His name,"*

*"...then **in my heart it becomes like a burning fire shut up in my bones, and I am weary of holding it in.** I cannot endure it."*

Job also said something similar in Job 32:18-20,

*"…for I am __full__ OF WORDS, __the spirit within me compels me__,"*

*"…behold indeed my belly* (my heart, my spirit) *__is like wine that has no vent__; like new wineskins __it is about to burst__."*

*"I __will__ speak that I may find relief; I __must__ open my mouth and answer."*

The two disciples on the road to Emmaus also experienced this:

*"__Did not our hearts burn within us__ while He talked with us on the road, and __while He opened the Scriptures to us?__"* - Luke 24:32.

Paul put it this way in 2Corinthians 4:13

*"…we have __the same spirit of faith__,"*
*That spirit of faith is "__according to what is written__,"*

*"I believed __and therefore__ I spoke,"*

*"…__just so, according to what is written, "we also believe and therefore speak__…"*

What was it that the apostles,

*"…__saw and heard__"* …that caused them to speak?

1John 1 says that,

*"...it was the word of LIFE,"*

(It was the word concerning eternal LIFE,

...concerning the LIFE of God,

...concerning the abundant LIFE,

...which was promised from before time began,

...by God Himself who cannot lie (Titus 1:2)

...by God our Daddy who loves us;

...it was that LIFE,

...that very LIFE of LOVE we enjoyed between us and the Father)

*"...which was manifested..."*

The word of LIFE was manifested,

(...revealed, made known, *"opened"*) to them.

They saw and heard and believed

*"The Word of LIFE;"*

*"The Word of His Grace;"*

*"The Word of TRUTH;"*

*"The Word of REDEMPTION;"*

*"The Word of His LOVE and how He came in person and RESCUED US"*

So there in the gospel of John we read about **this eternal LIFE and LOVE.**

It says there that,

*"...it became flesh and dwelt among us and we beheld His glory"*

...**we beheld the glory of that LIFE and of His LOVE for US!**

In verse 4 John says that,

*"...this LIFE is the true light* **(it is the TRUTH)** *that gives light* **(revelation, understanding)** *to Man* **(concerning our origin; concerning our true design; concerning our Daddy's love and fondness of us.)"**

**I believe it is absolutely vital then for us to make a study of this LIFE; this GLORY; this LIGHT; this TRUTH; this LOVE;**

For it is **the strategy of God revealed,**

...**to ignite the Church with passion to reach the world,**

It is **the strategy of God revealed,**

*...to win the world over to Him,*

*"...for it gives light* (real truth, real enlightenment, real understanding, real freedom) *to mankind"*

**It is the very understanding mankind needs** *to return to their original design,*

*...and return to God their true Father,*

*...and enjoy abundant LIFE.*

# Chapter 6

## The glory of the Lord

The prophets of old prophesied about this
**"Word of Life"** becoming <u>the light</u> (the true
enlightenment) of men (of mankind; every
person on the face of the earth).

Isaiah 40:1-8

1 *"Comfort, yes, comfort my people!' says your
God."*

2 *'Speak comfort to Jerusalem,* **and cry out to
her that her warfare is ended**,*"*

**(Her struggle against the devil; against
sin's rule; the struggle within themselves,
even against themselves, is ended),**

*"...**tell her that her iniquity <u>is</u> pardoned**;"*

*"...**<u>for</u> she has received from the Lord's
hand <u>double</u> for <u>all</u> her sins.**"*

He goes on to say:

3 *"...the voice of one crying in the wilderness:
Prepare the way of the Lord; Make straight, <u>in
the desert</u>, a highway for our God.'*

Then he begins to declare (Now notice the detail; how thorough; how complete this work of redemption):

4 *"**Every** valley **shall** be exalted, and **every** mountain and hill **shall** be made low; the crooked places **shall** be made straight, and the rough places smooth;"*

How shall this happen?

5 *"**The glory of the Lord**..."*

**(The DOXA - The nature of God; The weight of who He is; His very person, the very weight of His opinion; the substance of His truth concerning Himself and concerning us; His accurate estimation of our true value and worth; that very glory we lost in the garden; our original identity; our true design; the very image and likeness of God within us)**

*"...**shall be REVEALED** (in Jesus Christ and proclaimed in the gospel),"*

*"...and all flesh **shall see** it (shall be attracted to it and grasp it; and understand it; and literally behold it and experience it and physically see it with their own eyes)"*

*"...**for the mouth of the Lord has spoken**."*

6 *"The voice said 'Cry out!'*

*...and he said, 'What shall I cry?'*

*'All flesh is as grass* (fragile and at best temporary), *and **all its loveliness** (its glory) is like the flower of the field."*

7 *"The grass withers* (it's a fact), *the flower fades* (inevitable),*"*

*"...**UNLESS the Breath of the Lord blows upon it**;"*

*"**Surely the people are grass**."*

8 *"The grass withers* (it's a fact), *the flower fades* (inevitable),*"*

*"**BUT** the Word of our God..."*

(*"**The word of His grace;**" "**The word of TRUTH;**" "**The word of LIFE;**" "**The Word of His LOVE for us;**" "**His value, His estimation of our worth; His revelation and declaration of our original design and true identity**"*)

**That glory; That Word** *"**endures forever!**"*

Can you see the distinct detail and design of this highway *God has built in Christ's work of redemption?*

*...*and wants to build through us *who see and understand these things?*

He wants to extend His knowledge; His resources; His gospel; His grace; His very LOVE *into the desert of human experience and existence!*

It includes *every area!*

Every area; *every desert area of human life!*

4 *"**Every** valley **shall** be exalted, and **every** mountain and hill **shall** be made low; the crooked places **shall** be made straight, and the rough places smooth;"*

Listen, God wants to make our lives and our mouths a highway for His word in a very practical way;

...for the revealing and communication of His TRUTH; for the revealing and communication of His LOVE!

...but before we even try to reveal it and communicate it with our mouths He wants His word to first have such entrance into our own hearts and lives and our own thinking, *that it deals with every area,*

...so that our lives may become a vehicle for His word ...a highway for God, into a desert land,

...so that He can take the water of the word of His LOVE *straight into the lives of those who are dying without that water*

He says, there in verse 4,

*"**Every** valley **shall** be exalted, and **every** mountain and hill **shall** be made low; the crooked places **shall** be made straight, and the rough places smooth;"*

Peter says in 2Peter 1:19 that;

*"…we have the prophetic word* (…the word about the work of grace, God's promise of LIFE) *…**made more sure*** (…that means it came to pass)*"

*"…which you do well to **heed** as a light that shines in a dark place,"*

*"UNTIL the day dawns* (…or SO THAT the day may dawn; so that **revelation may come**)*"*

*"…and the morning star* (...insight and understanding; and the bright manifestation of God's truth and glory; the true light; the Christ-life) *…rises* (…and reigns) *…in your hearts;"*

Isaiah says, and I paraphrase,

*"…**all the nations are as grass and will wither and fade without the breath of the Lord blowing on them**."*

The *"**breath of the Lord**"* speaks of **the influence of the Spirit of God, through the word of the Gospel; that influence of the love of God** that lives and abides forever.

I want you to notice that **God needs us for His plan to be fulfilled.**

**WE** are the highway of God and **without the breath of God blowing through us upon the nations,** *they will surely perish.*

**We are His hands and feet, and His mouth.**

**We are His body; the only means** *through which to express Himself* **here on earth!**

# Chapter 7

## Making an impact

Turn with me now to Isaiah 60:1-3 and *hear the appeal and promise of God to us,* His Church (His EKKLESIA); His called out ones; the ones who understand the call; *those who see and understand and believe these things;* His dwelling place; His body; His expression of Himself; His very hands and feet and mouth;

He says:

1 *"Arise, shine; <u>for your LIGHT</u> **has come!** And* **the GLORY** *OF THE LORD* **<u>is</u>** <u>risen upon you</u>*."*

2 *"For behold,* **the** *darkness…*

(…the lies and deception that has ruled us since Adam's fall; Sin and all its ugly consequences) **shall cover the earth**,*"*

*"…and* **deep** *darkness the people…*

(…ignorance, confusion, deception, missing the mark, living outside our design, these things shall be prevalent, big time!)

*"**BUT** THE LORD WILL ARISE OVER YOU, and **HIS GLORY** <u>WILL BE SEEN UPON YOU</u>."*

3 *"The gentiles **SHALL** COME TO **YOUR LIGHT**, and kings to **THE BRIGHTNESS** OF YOUR RISING."*

Listen carefully,

*"Our light **has come;**"*

*"…the glory of the Lord **is risen** upon us"*

…**and not even the devil could stop it from coming to pass!**

**Hallelujah!**

**I tell you; the devil has a problem!**

*He cannot reverse what God has revealed and what God has said!*

**The LIFE was manifested,**

…**it came just as God promised,**

…**and now that light gives light and truth and enlightenment to every man!**

*…and the devil cannot stop it from happening,*

*…just as much as darkness cannot overpower the light,*

*…or prevent it from shining,*

*…or stop its influence.*

104

**Aren't you glad God's Word (what God has revealed and spoken to us in Jesus)** *is more powerful than the devil and his forces of darkness any day?*

The devil cannot stop God's Word; God's Gospel, from making an impact,

…**because Almighty God is there to watch over His word, to perform it!**

Can you see that!

**History couldn't stop the prophetic word from coming to pass!**

**Not even history itself can erase God's guarantee He places on His word.**

**There are not enough laps of time in all of time to diminish God's word, nor its energy and power, in any way,**

…**because God's word is every bit as eternal as God Himself!**

**God watches over His word;** *over the promise of LOVE and LIFE attached to the gospel,* <u>to bring it to pass</u>!

*…*<u>He empowers it</u>!

The devil would have to kill God to stop His word from being eternal in nature, or from having power,

…and he doesn't have a snowball's chance in hell of ever doing that.

Ha… ha… ha…

**To say that God is more powerful than the devil, *is an extreme understatement!***

**There is NO comparison!**

**That is why *The Word of Life* that comes to us in the gospel is more powerful than Satan,**

**…just as light (even just a little bit of light) is more powerful *than all the darkness put together!***

**Listen, darkness does not have real power; it is not actually a force; *it is merely the absence of a force,* LIGHT.**

**Just like a lie or deception only has power and influence *as long as THE TRUTH is obscured.***

Have you ever lit a match in a dark room?

What happens?

**The darkness has to flee before it.**

**I say again: *Satan has a problem!***

**Hallelujah!**

He couldn't stop *The Word of Life and LOVE* from taking on flesh in Jesus Christ and becoming manifested.

He also cannot stop *The Word of Life and LOVE* from becoming manifested in us.

He cannot reverse what *God* <u>has spoken</u>.

He cannot cancel what *God* says even still today.

<u>*God's* Word</u> does not return to Him void!

All of history couldn't stop *the prophetic Word* from coming to pass.

<u>*God's* Word of Life and LOVE</u> was manifested *in all its glory!*

...and now <u>*God's* Word of Life and LOVE</u> <u>shall accomplish</u> what *God* sent it out to do *in us and through us!*

In Hebrews 1:3 we read concerning Jesus; concerning *The Word of Life and LOVE* that became manifested:

*"...who <u>being</u> **the brightness <u>of His glory</u>** and the **expressed image of His person**..."*

When *"The Word of Life and LOVE"* was manifested ***in all its glory***, we read in John 11:48 that the Pharisees (the religious leaders; religious people) conspired against Jesus.

They were filled with jealousy and rage.

They saw Him as a threat.

**They were intimidated by _the brightness of His glory_.**

**He was undoing their deception; their doctrines; half-truths; even outright lies.**

They wanted control and influence and power, and they tried to compete with Him _for the hearts and the minds of the people._

They said:

_"**If we let Him alone like this, (if we keep letting Him have His influence), everyone will believe in Him**, and then the Romans will come and take away both our place and the nation."_

(They were not only afraid of riots, and of the people proclaiming Jesus the new King of the Jews, _but they were also afraid of losing their place of authority among the people, they were fighting to preserve their format of religion, their rituals and traditions, and even the very identity of their nation because of their religion, and especially their own identity that was wrapped up in their religion._

They were afraid their religious rituals and traditions; their form of godliness, will be put out of its place, it will be displaced and put out of commission.

***BUT most of all, they were afraid of losing their income from the religious system they have built and relied upon and had their identity in.***)

In John 12:19 **they had to admit that they took on more than they had bargained for.**

They decided to kill this Jesus, because **they didn't know what else to do to stop *the brightness of His glory* from impacting the hearts of people.**

They didn't know what they were dealing with.

**They were fighting a force far stronger than them:**

*"The Pharisees therefore said among themselves, '**You see that you are accomplishing nothing. Look, <u>the whole world has gone after Him</u>!**"*

**You see the life and LOVE Jesus lived *was our original design on display;* the fact that *we are actually children of God;* His image; His likeness in the flesh.**

**The life and LOVE Jesus lived in the flesh; the same flesh we have, *was our true identity on exhibit.***

He lived in the flesh, the life of *true freedom*, of *irresistible LOVE* and *deep intimate friendship* with the living, eternal, miracle working God,

…whom He called and knew as *Father,*

"…*OUR Father…*"

…<u>and therefore His life was *very attractive!*</u>

# Chapter 8

## *Missing out on God's plan*

This attraction to Jesus' irresistible LIFE (*to the source of His life and love*) can be clearly seen in the account of the Greeks who came a long way just to meet Him.

John 12:20-36,

20 *"Now there were certain Greeks,* (who came all the way from somewhere in Greece, or Galatia, perhaps Ephesus, but probably Antioch …they were) *among those who came up to worship at the feast."*

21 *"Then they came to Philip, who was from Bethsaida of Galilee, and asked him, saying,* **'Sir, we wish to see Jesus.***"*

22 *"Phillip came and told Andrew, and in turn Andrew and Phillip told Jesus."*

You see I want you to notice that those Greeks, even though they were coming from afar off were not interested in the Jewish religious festival.

They did not come for the Jewish festival.

They didn't come to see religion on display;

No, **they came to see Jesus; *The Word of Life and TRUTH and LOVE* on display.**

This is a very important, but often overlooked, lesson.

It is still the same today as it was then:

**People don't want religion; *they can see it's nothing but empty legalistic bondage;***

**...they can see that it is at best just an empty form of Godliness *that has no real power to set anybody free.***

**It has no *real* LIFE; no *real* LOVE in it; nothing *REAL* in it.**

***People want that which is REAL;***

***...they don't want anything fake!***

***They want to see this eternal life, this abundant LIFE; this abundant LOVE we were designed for, <u>on display FOR REAL in us</u>!***

So, those Greeks came a long way to see Jesus;

***...to see The Word of LIFE and TRUTH and LOVE on display,***

**BUT they still missed it.**

**They still missed** *what <u>God</u> wanted to say to them in the life of this man Jesus.*

Oh... how we *all* have missed it!

How we *all* have missed **what *God* has to say to us** *in Jesus!*

You see, as powerful as *The Word of God* is, yet Jesus said in Matthew 15:6

*"...you have made The Word of God <u>of no effect in your life</u> by your traditions, inherited from your forefathers* (from their futile ways)*."*

And so those Greeks came all that way, you see, they weren't interested in religion,

*…*they weren't interested in the Jewish religious festival; they came to see Jesus, not the festival,

*…*BUT what they didn't realize was that they too inherited customs and traditions, a way of thinking, *futile, sentimental, religious nonsense thinking,* from their forefathers,

*…***and it was about to make them loose out on seeing Jesus.**

When they arrived they went to Andrew and Philip and said:

113

*"Sirs, we wish to see Jesus,"*

Andrew and Phillip *probably thought that this was great* that those Greeks came all that long way to see Jesus.

*Their Master was now really starting to become popular and,*

**...fame was theirs at last.**

**They could clearly picture how the ministry could now go global,**

**...and they would be launched with it!**

The Scripture goes on to say that,

*"...they went and told Jesus,"*

And I can just imagine what they and some of the others could have been thinking and strategizing;

*'Jesus, please don't disappoint these people now, please give them what they want, they came all this way for a show, just to be entertained by You!'*

*'Can't you just quickly tickle their ears with one of your beautiful sayings, and maybe do a miracle or two for them?'*

*'...and You know already, that if it's real good Jesus, they will surely spread the word, and*

114

*who knows, they might just give us a good offering as well…'*

**If this was really their attitude they sure missed it big time!**

*…**Jesus and the Father had much more in mind than that.***

You see the Greeks could have been touched *emotionally.*

They could have had their *special treatment;*

*…*they could have had a service *catered specifically for them,*

*…**they could have experienced the anointing, and they could have seen their miracle!***

They could have gone home, ***very excited,*** *with a huge testimony;*

*'Oh, our own eyes have seen His glory!'*

*'Oh, wasn't that wonderful!'*

**BUT it would have benefited them *from very little to nothing*!**

Why do I say that?

**Because they would have *missed the whole purpose of God for their lives***

*...because after a while the glory of that experience would have faded and they would have needed another fix,*

*...another experience to bring back the goose bumps.*

They would have had to go *to yet another city, to yet another meeting,*

*...and what if Jesus had left by then, or they couldn't find Him?*

That whole wonderful *euphoria,* that whole wonderful *feeling;* that whole *wonderful experience* **would have been gone in just a few short months, or weeks even,**

*...***and then they would have ended up *just as hungry and thirsty and unfulfilled, and just as unsatisfied with life* as they were before they went to see Jesus.**

**They would have been left with *only a memory* of a wonderful experience, *and even the memory of it would begin to fade after a while*...**

*'...What was that again we experienced in Jerusalem?'*

*'...We remember that anointing, it felt wonderful,'*

*'...but maybe it wasn't all that great,'*

116

*'…after all there are many who now say that this Jesus was a phony and a fraud!'*

They would have ended up *maybe even more cynical* than they were before Jesus came along,

*…just like so many people today that have been disappointed by this whole Christian religion thing.*

Let me tell you, Jesus had much more in mind for them *than just a touch from the anointing,* just *a fading experience;*

*…*a wonderful, *but <u>fading</u> experience!*

Hey listen, God is not out *to entertain us* with His word!!!!

He has more in mind for us than just a wonderful, *but fading experience,* in our encounter of His word; *of His gospel.*

God wants His word and His gospel to have a permanent, life altering, LIFE giving impact upon our lives.

And listen, He has <u>a greater purpose</u> for our gatherings together around His word *than just <u>our</u> edification.*

Listen to how Jesus responded when the Greeks asked to see Him:

John 12:23 & 24

23 *"…But Jesus answered them, saying,*

**'The hour has come that the <u>son of MAN</u> should be GLORIFIED…"**

I want you to notice:

Jesus said, **"<u>son of MAN</u>,"** not Son of God,

He said: **"<u>son of MAN</u>,"** meaning MANKIND!

**…because Jesus didn't just represent God the Father;**

**…He also represented mankind itself.**

**He was God and man <u>united in one body</u>,**

**…and He didn't come to start yet another religion,**

**…He came to redeem and restore the image and likeness of God in Man;**

**…the LIFE and LOVE of God restored, in fallen humanity!**

**…that very LIFE and LOVE we were designed to experience and express!**

**He came to seek and to save that which was lost!**

He came to reconcile God's kids back unto Him; *back to their true Daddy!*

He said:

23 *"The hour has come that the <u>son of MAN</u> should be GLORIFIED."*

24 *"Most assuredly, I say to you, unless a grain of wheat falls into the ground and dies, it remains alone;"*

*"...<u>but if it dies, IT PRODUCES MUCH GRAIN</u>"*

*"...MUCH <u>GRAIN!</u>"*

*The <u>same</u> quality!*

*...the <u>exact same</u> kind,*

*...<u>reproduced and multiplied</u>!*

Jesus was very conscious of *the legal and very vital implications* of His death.

He knew that *the <u>ONLY way</u> He could possibly impact the nations* was to *reproduce His very own LIFE and LOVE;*

*...His very own enjoyment of abundant LIFE;*

*...His very own GLORY,*

*...which is the light of Man!*

*...the true* LIFE and LOVE and FRIENDSHIP and PRESENCE and POWER OF GOD *that Man was designed for,*

*...to reproduce it in Philip, Andrew, Peter

*...and everyone *who has an ear to hear* <u>and a heart to believe</u>,

*...and TREASURE *"The word of LIFE."*

Hebrews 1:1 & 2 says that,

1 *"God, who at various times in the past, and in different ways* (in fragments of thought and prophetic shadows and pictures,) *spoke, in time past, to the fathers, by the prophets,"*

2 *"...**has** in <u>these</u> last days* (in the fullness of time) ***spoken to us in HIS SON***..."

Listen, God desires for His word; for Jesus,

*...He desires for what *is being said in His Word,* (for *what is being said in Jesus,* in His LIFE, in the very LIFE and LOVE of Jesus) <u>to become our experience</u>.

In Jesus God has spoken SON to us!

There's a message in the Son; TRUTH, the truth about our origin, about our true identity, about our sonship,

120

...about our redemption and restoration and reconciliation with our true Father, our Daddy God, *is revealed in Him!*

God wants sonship, the LIFE and LOVE of a son; of His very own dear children to be revealed *though our lives also,* just as it was revealed in Jesus;

...*and that includes the supernatural power of God exhibited in Jesus' life.*

Listen, God wants <u>*His*</u> *Word,* flesh in YOU!

The fullness of God, the fullness of the LIFE and LOVE and POWER of God;

...that *original design and true identity we were designed in and made for, which was on display in the flesh, in Jesus,*

...*displayed also in your heart and life* is the strategy of God to reach this world.

You see every person is designed for that LIFE and LOVE and POWER ENCOUNTER with the Spirit of God,

...and when they see it enjoyed and lived before them, and hear it spoken about to them, *their hearts cannot help but to respond and bear witness with it.*

From within them, *their own hearts begin to cry out to them* that this LIFE and LOVE and

SPIRIT POWER spoken of and plainly lived, exhibited before them, *is what they were designed for.*

We can have great confidence in our witness to mankind,

...because every person's heart *is custom designed for LOVE!*

It's *custom designed to respond* when it hears THE TRUTH of its design and origin in God,

...*and no person can easily escape their own heart; their own spirit.*

Therefore shall no person who heard THE TRUTH, *and still refuse to respond to LOVE* have any excuse before God either!

...because *when we hear and see* THE GOSPEL *on display,* with POWER,

...faith comes with it *automatically,*

...and the Holy Spirit of God *bears strong witness with it* in our hearts.

In order for people to be able to continue to ignore these things, you actually have to resist THE TRUTH, resist the SPIRIT OF GOD; resist LOVE HIMSELF, *speaking in your spirit.*

Romans 10:17 says that

*"...faith **COMES** by hearing... the WORD OF GOD,"*

**So a person *actually has to reject the faith that comes into their heart* when they hear THE GOSPEL in order to *not* be influenced and transformed by it.**

**Therefore, we preach and live it *with great boldness and confidence!***

In John 12:36 we read,

*"While you have the light, **believe** in the light, that you may **become** sons* (actual authentic inevitable byproducts, naturally reproduced byproducts) *of the light."*

*"**These things Jesus spoke, and then departed from them and went and hid himself from them."***

Why did Jesus do that?

I say again:

*...it is because He had more in mind than entertaining them with His love and the anointing.*

**God has *much more in mind for us* that just to entertain us on a Sunday morning with the latest word from the pulpit.**

Don't be like those Greeks when it comes to encountering *The Gospel of God …**what God has to say to you in Christ Jesus!***

Don't allow yourself to just be entertained by THE LIGHT, (…by *"The word of His grace;"* by *"The word of TRUTH and LOVE and BELONGING")* …**it is the gospel; it is good news; *it is the truth of where you truly come from, and where you truly belong, and of what has happened in Christ Jesus to totally restore you back to the Father and your original design, and to completely bless and benefit you in every possible way.***

**Absorb THE LIGHT; absorb THE TRUTH**, *so your heart can find a home* and *so you can become **true light** in the world;*

*…**true light** in the midst of a crooked and perverse generation.*

*…**true light** even in a compromising politically correct world;*

*…**true light** to an ignorant, confused and deceived world;*

**Unless *"the GLORY"* gets restored to them**, *by the breath of God; by the Spirit and TRUTH and LOVE of God, **made manifest in our lives and coming forth from our mouths,** **they will remain unfulfilled,** without hope, without God in this world.

All that remain for them in life is to wither like wild flowers and fade away like grass and to be thrown into the fire and be destroyed by life and by circumstances and by the enemy.

**Treasure *The Word of Life* and TRUTH and LOVE in your heart *and live it out loud!***

**Don't have a casual attitude, just wanting to be entertained, *just wanting to feel the joy and the goose bumps for yourself.***

**God has more in mind for you *than just a touch* of the anointing, *just an emotional encounter* in a church gathering, *just another religious experience.***

**God has more than religion in mind for us.**

So many people come to meetings to see a man of God skilled with the word, doing miracles …**but they fail to see that the Father *also desires for them to walk in that REALITY and to set the captives free*,**

…for according to Ephesians 1:20, and 2:6

*"He raised Him* (Jesus) *from the dead and seated Him at and in and as His right hand in the heavenly places, FAR ABOVE **all** principality and power and might and dominion, and every name that is named…"*

*"…**and He raised us up together with Him, and made us sit** (together with Him in a*

place of authority; we are seated in Him,) *together with Him* (sharing His executive authority) *in the heavenly places,* (we are) *in Christ Jesus."*

Treasure *"The word of LIFE."*

Believe and embrace and treasure THIS TRUTH, this REALITY in your heart!

Jesus said in Matthew 6:22

*"...If the eye* (your vision; what you see; your focus; what you believe) *is single (...*is accurate)*"*

(...He is talking about a clear understanding;

...He is talking about having a single minded clear focus upon *The Word of Truth; The Gospel of YOUR Salvation,*

...just like the focus a broody hen has towards her eggs.

...If you treasure *"The word of LIFE,"* if you treasure *"The word of TRUTH and LOVE,"* if you are single minded, fully persuaded),

*"...then your whole body will be full of light..."*

(...your whole mind and being; your whole spirit, will be full of understanding, full of TRUTH, full of faith, full of abundant life, *real* LIFE, *real* anointing, *real* power, *real* freedom, *real* joy, *real* peace, *real* LOVE, *real* fulfillment).*"*

**Hallelujah!**

Read Isaiah 60:1-3 again

*"Arise, shine; for YOUR LIGHT **has come!**"*

*"And the GLORY OF THE LORD **has** risen upon YOU…"*

*"…**the** darkness* (the lies and deception that has been passed on to us through Adam, through his fall; Sin and all its ugly consequences) *shall cover the earth, and **deep** darkness the people* (ignorance, confusion, deception, missing the mark; living outside of their true identity and original design)*;"*

*"…**BUT** THE LORD WILL ARISE OVER YOU,"*

*"…and **HIS GLORY** WILL BE SEEN UPON YOU."*

*"The gentiles **SHALL** COME TO **YOUR LIGHT**,"*

*"…and kings to **THE BRIGHTNESS** OF **YOUR RISING**."*

**Can you see that there is something about the <u>brightness</u> of <u>our rising</u> that kings**

**cannot ignore, and the nations cannot resist!**

Let's return to John 12 and let's read verse 37

*"**BUT although** (even though) He had done **so many** signs before them, **they did not believe in Him**."*

*They enjoyed that emotional encounter; they were thrilled by the experience, **BUT the void remained.***

Why?

Because you see *they fed only upon that which the senses could offer,*

*(...**instead of feeding upon THE WORD; and the LOVE in that word, and absorbing it, believing it, embracing it and becoming one with it,**)*

*...**therefore** the void remained.*

**You see; the void can only be filled by FAITH!**

**The void can only be filled by LOVE!**

**You can feed on all that the senses can offer you, *but the void will remain in your heart and life* when The Word is not your sustaining substance and your life.**

In Job 28 we read about Man's search for satisfaction.

Job describes how men everywhere *knows that life must be **more than** just food or clothing, **more than** just eating wheat.*

He describes how they begin to dig up the mountains *looking for something more,*

### *...looking for something to treasure*

He describes how it's Man's desire *for something of greater value* that drives him to overturn mountains seeking for treasure.

They are looking for **true** treasure.

Man's **drive** for **true** treasure, Man's **need** for **true satisfaction** is **so great** *he will leave no stone unturned, no avenue unexplored, **not even the depth of sin.***

Why is there **such a drive** in Man for this ever-elusive **true** treasure?

**And don't kid yourself there <u>is</u> a DRIVE for that *true* treasure, *even in YOU!***

It is because deep within our hearts all of mankind knows that **there has got to be more to life**.

We all know that,

*"**Life is more** than food and clothing,"*
                                                          *- Matthew 6:25*

We act the way we do because our condition *has spiritual roots,* whether we know it or not,

*…or whether we want to admit it or not.*

**You see unconsciously we are all searching for true fulfillment;**

**…we are searching for that GLORY, that LIFE; that LOVE,**

**…that GLORIOUS LIFE of our original design and identity;**

**…that LIFE WITH GOD that Man fell from in the Garden of Eden.**

**Man's spirit is starving for righteousness; *for oneness with God;* for enjoying <u>the love and acceptance of God</u>;**

**…the very glory we once had in the garden.**

Jesus spoke **the truth** when He said in Luke 12:15,

*"**One's life does not consist in** the abundance of things he possess,"*

But Satan has blinded us about our **true** need and deceived us about what will bring about **true satisfaction**.

130

If Satan can keep us busy pursuing after *false* or *inferior* treasure like the lusts of the flesh, or the lust of the eyes, or the pride of life; worldly riches and things like recognition and prestige and power and influence;

...if he can keep us busy pursuing the flesh, he can keep us from finding *true* satisfaction.

Isaiah 55:1-3

1 *"Ho!"*

(God is trying to get our attention! He wants us to stop dead in our tracks, *because we are going the wrong way!*)

*"Everyone who* (spiritually) *thirsts, Come to the waters* (the voice of God, the Word of God, the TRUTH and LOVE of God);

*"...and you who have no money* (you who have come to the end of yourself), *Come, buy* (with **understanding;** with **insight**; with **faith**, which is the currency of heaven) *and eat* (find **satisfaction**).*"*

*"Yes, come; buy* (with **faith**) *wine* (the influence of the Spirit) *and milk* (the nourishment that comes from your Source; from the sustenance of the Word of Truth; from God's LOVE FOR YOU) *without money and without price."*

(These things are beyond value; you cannot put a price on it; **it is priceless and precious; it is treasure beyond compare!**)

2 *"Why do you spend money* (Why do you even consider the value of something, weigh out silver, reason within yourself, trying to contend, and fight) *for what is not bread"*

(…in other words why do you waste your life, **for what does not sustain your life**),

*"…and your wages* (your labor, your energy, your passion, your drive, what you are worth) *for what does not* **(permanently, truly) satisfy?"**

*"***Listen diligently to Me, and eat** *what is* (truly) *good"*

(He is talking about His Word, about the work of redemption; He is talking about the TRUTH and LOVE of God;

He is talking about the gospel that reveals our origin, design and true identity, as well as our friendship with God, *restored to us in Jesus Christ*)

*"…and let your* **soul delight itself (become satisfied)** *in abundance* (the abundance of His love and acceptance; this place of belonging and of family and intimate friendship and fellowship with God)."*

3 *"**Incline your ear,** and come to Me* (begin a relationship with Me through BELIEVING The Word; through **embracing** My TRUTH and **embracing** My LOVE)*."*

*"**HEAR (UNDERSTAND), and your soul shall live**;"*

*"And I will make an **everlasting** covenant* (commitment and permanent connection) *with you"*

Romans 3:23 makes it clear why we all need to listen diligently,

*"...For there is no difference; **for ALL** have sinned,* (have missed the mark, and lived outside of their design)*"*

*"...**have fallen short of the GLORY** of God."*

We all need the LIFE that is, **revealed and given to us as a gift**, in the *"Word of His Grace;"* the *"Gospel of our Salvation and Redemption and Restoration."*

Romans 3:24 go on to say that,

*"...we all* (who have sinned, and lost our way, and fell short of the glory...) ***we all, have been justified freely by His grace (as a gift)**;"*

*"...**through the redemption that is already given to us in Christ Jesus**"*

...It was by His work of Redemption; *by Christ Jesus and God the Father Himself, by their doing* on that cross and in that resurrection and ascension!

This justification of life; this being made right again; this being made righteous; this restoration and acceptance and being made whole again *was given to us freely AS A GIFT* in that work of redemption!

...all we have to do is BELIEVE it;

...EMBRACE it; EMBRACE THE TRUTH and be PERSUADED in it;

...in our heart, not just our head,

...TREASURE it in other words;

...allow it to TRANSFORM our way of thinking;

...allow it to RENEW OUR MINDS and TRANSFORM our HEART and our SPIRIT and our very CONDUCT,

...allow ourselves to BE RENEWED in the SPIRIT of our MINDS and our VERY WAY OF LIFE!

# Chapter 9

## Consider the Real glory

Let's read Isaiah 40:6-8 again,

6 *"Cry aloud! ...What shall I cry?*

*'**All flesh is grass, and all its loveliness** (its accomplishments, its reputation, <u>its glory</u>) **is like the flower of the field**.'*

7 *"***(Surely the people are grass) *the grass withers, the flower fades <u>UNLESS the breath of the Lord blows upon them</u>.*"

8 *"The grass withers, the flower fades;* **BUT The Word of our God** *endures forever* (it never diminishes in strength and beauty and attraction; its **glory** never fades, it contains eternal TRUTH and LIFE for **it is <u>God</u> breathed**)*"

**That breath of life is hidden in The Word of the Gospel for us to find,**

*…***that we might partake of its GLORY; it's TRUTH; it's LOVE**

*…***and truly *live!***

Let's also read John 12:23 & 38 again,

*"**The hour has come** that the **son of MAN should be GLORIFIED**..."*

*"...that the word of Isaiah the prophet might be fulfilled, which he spoke: ...And **to whom has the arm of the Lord been revealed?**"*

What was this *"**hour**"* that Jesus was talking about?

What was *"**the arm of the Lord**"* revealed?

Jesus was quoting Isaiah 53.

Let us read there from verse 3-6.

(It is prophetically speaking about Jesus' substitutionary sacrifice **on our behalf**, about the **legal and very vital implications** of Jesus' death; **about what He accomplished for us on the cross**).

Isaiah 53:3-12,

3 *"He was **despised and rejected** by men* (by mankind, not just the Jews), *a man of sorrows* (pain - a deep burden because of Man's sin) *and acquainted* (he knew it well) *with grief* (sickness - spiritual and therefore also physical)."*

*"We* (mankind) *hid, as it were, our faces from Him;* (we did not even give Him a second look)

136

*He was despised, and* **we did not esteem Him** (we did not see His real worth or significance),

*"BUT…"*

Then he goes on to explain by what he means that the Messiah would be,

*"…a man of sorrows, acquainted with grief."*

4 *"**BUT surely** He has borne* **OUR GRIEFS** (our spiritual sickness) *and carried* **OUR SORROWS** (our pain because of sin; our very sin itself); **yet we esteemed Him stricken, smitten by God, and afflicted**.*"

(We in our religious upbringing and mindsets thought He was afflicted with demons, we thought He was stricken by God for blasphemy, we thought God was smiting Him on that cross for His own sins)

5 *"**BUT** He was WOUNDED* **FOR OUR** *TRANSGRESSIONS; He was BRUISED* **FOR OUR** *INIQUITIES;"*

*"…the chastisement* **FOR OUR** *PEACE was upon Him, and BY HIS STRIPES* **WE ARE** *HEALED,"*

6 *"**All we** like sheep* **have gone astray; we have turned, every one, to his own way**;"*

*"**BUT** the Lord* **has laid on Him** *the iniquity of* **US ALL**."*

7 *"He was oppressed and He was afflicted, yet He opened not His mouth* (...in protest. He took it willingly, because He loves us; because **we needed** salvation; we needed to be redeemed and restored back to our original design and true identity and place of belonging in the bosom of our Father God, of our Daddy);*"*

*"He was led as a lamb to the slaughter..."*

8 *"...For He was cut off from the land of the living; **for the transgression of My people**..."*

(God was talking about **all of us** not just the Jews. He was talking prophetically. God calls **all of us, the whole human race**; *"My people,"*

...because *"the earth is the Lord's and the fullness thereof; the world and those that dwell therein"* – Psalm 24

He is our Maker, our Daddy; we belong to Him; we belong with Him; we belong in His family!)

*"...**for the transgression <u>of My people</u> He was stricken.**"*

10 *"...it pleased the Lord to bruise* (crush) *Him;"*

Why?

**Because He loves us!**

**He did it for us!**

*"He has put Him to grief* (**He made His soul an offering for sin**.)

11 *"...**By His knowledge** (by <u>this</u> "Word of Truth,"* by <u>this</u> "Word of His grace," by <u>this</u> "Word of Life and Truth and Love and Acceptance and Belonging") *My righteous Servant* (Jesus) **shall justify (the) many. (He shall justify the many, [all of us, the whole human race])** *for He* **shall bear <u>their</u> iniquities.**"

12 *"...He shall divide the spoil* (restore the lost glory back unto us), **because He poured out His soul unto death, and** (because) **He was numbered with the transgressors, and** (because) **He bore the sin of the many** (the whole human race)**, and made intercession for** (stood in the place of) **the transgressors (all of us**.)"

Jesus said,

*"...the hour has come for the **son of MAN** to be GLORIFIED!"*

**To be glorified means to be restored to what we were designed for; to be restored to the LIFE of God; FRIENDSHIP with the living miracle working God;**

**...to be restored to our original true identity and intimate relationship as His dear children; His very own offspring,**

**...to be restored to THAT life,**

**...that's what it means to be glorified.**

The apostle Peter says in 1 Peter 1:10-12 that,

10 "(Of this time, and of this person; of the Messiah; of the Christ and) *Of **THIS SALVATION** the prophets have inquired and searched diligently, who prophesied **of this grace**"*

*...**that has now come to you**,"*

11 *"they were searching to find out **what exactly** and for **what time**, the Spirit of Christ, who was in them, was indicating **when He testified beforehand of Christ's sufferings and told of THE GLORIES THAT WOULD FOLLOW**."*

12 *"To them it was revealed that, not to themselves, **BUT TO US they were ministering when they wrote about these things,***

**...which now (in other words, it is no longer still waiting to be fulfilled at a future time)***"*

*"...**which now have been reported** to you **through** those who have preached **The Gospel** to you"*

(GOSPEL: **the good news** of *who you are* and of *what has happened* to redeem and

140

rescue and restore you back to your original design and back to your true Father!)

*"...they have preached these things to you by the Holy Spirit sent from Heaven - things which even angels desire to look into."*

What does these subsequent *"**GLORIES**"* imply?

*"...**THE GLORIES THAT WOULD FOLLOW**?"*

*"...**the sufferings of Christ**?"*

I suggest to you that **THESE GLORIES that would follow the sufferings of Christ are all about the legal and very vital; the practical, very vitally applicable to your life, implications** of His suffering *on our behalf*.

**The legal implication of His suffering and *the subsequent glory* is the very content of *"The Word of His Grace;" "The Word of Truth;" "the Word of Life;" "the LOVE of God" "the GOSPEL" and "the Arm of the Lord revealed."***

**It is *God's* Strategy.**

**The legal implications of His suffering and the subsequent *"GLORIES,"***

*"THE GLORIES THAT WOULD FOLLOW,"*

...or come TO US as a result of His suffering, _is_ *God's strategy;*

...it is *God's plan* for Man revealed,

...*it is what He has in mind for every single believer;*

...*every single person who love Him,*

...*and there is no plan B.*

God desires to attract your neighbor through the visible evidence of His Glory that shines in YOUR LIFE;

...that shines in YOUR countenance;

...that shines in YOUR JOY;

...that shines in YOUR conduct;

...that shines in YOUR LOVE;

...that shines in YOUR conversation!!!

His GLORY (DOXA) is His design;

...His estimation of your value and your worth; His opinion, His TRUTH about you, *is His design* ...His favor upon you, His reputation of Himself and of you, of His nature in you, His very image and likeness in you, *is His design;*

*...*His love for you and in you, His very LIFE and PERSON and PRESENCE and LOVE in you, *is His design!*

So, *"ARISE and SHINE for YOUR light HAS come,"*

*"...the GLORY of the Lord HAS risen upon YOU!"*

Going back to John 12:41,

*"These things Isaiah said ...when he saw His glory and spoke of Him."*

What are *"these things"* Isaiah said,

*...*I mean what exactly did Isaiah say?

Verse 38:

*"Lord who has believed our report?"*

*"To whom has the arm of the Lord been revealed?"*

So, he said 2 things but he was asking only one question: He wanted to know

1. *"Lord, who has believed our report* (the prophetic word about Christ's work)*?"*

2. *"To whom has the arm of the Lord been revealed?"*

He sounded very disappointed.

Why was he so disappointed?

Israel's response *(really mankind's response, not just the Jew's response)* disappointed him.

**They frustrated the strategy of God,**

***…because they shut their ears and their hearts!***

**They would not see what God was trying to say and demonstrate to them in Christ.**

Let us not be like the rulers in John 12:42-46,

42 *"…**even among the rulers many believed** in Him, **but nevertheless** because of the Pharisees **they did not confess Him**, lest they should be put out of the synagogue;"*

43 *"**for they loved <u>the praise</u> of men more than <u>the praise</u> of God**"*

44 *"Then Jesus cried out and said, '**He who believes in Me**…"*

(**…in My love for them; in My grace; in the work of redemption and salvation and restoration I came to do in other words**),

*'He who believes in Me …**believes not in Me but in Him who sent Me** (to accomplish that mission)."*

144

45 *"And **He who sees Me sees Him who sent Me**."*

46 *"I have come **as a light** (to bring revelation) **into the world**,"*

*"...that whoever believes in Me (*...in my love; in My grace; in the work of redemption I was sent to do)

*"...should not abide in darkness (*...should no longer have to continue in ignorance, confusion and a life of sin [missing the mark; living outside of their design]).*"*

But these people still chose to abide in darkness.

Because, *"...they **loved** the praise of men **more than** the praise of God"* - John 12:43

That word *"**praise**"* can also be translated *"**glory**."*

So this Scripture could also read:

*"...they loved the **glory of men** more than the **glory of God**."*

In other words, **they loved what they could see in Man, and were taught by the Fall of Man, and their own experience, and the religious opinions of Man, *more than* what *they could see and hear in Christ*.**

I have explained this word before, but it is such a rich word in its meaning that I am going to explain it again in the light of this Scripture

…and I am going to keep emphasizing it in this book, as I also do in many of my other books, because it is such a key word for us to understand the depth of meaning of.

The word *"glory"* comes from the Greek word: - DOXA or DOKEO, and **it refer to having a reputation (to render or esteem glorious.)**

It speaks of being full of, or having glory, honor, and dignity.

The words: - *worship, praise, admiration and respect come to mind.*

It speaks of what is *very apparent* (*radiant,* in other words; *it shines forth; it is beautiful; it is glorious*).

*It not only speaks of God's presence and person,* though,

(…His love, His Life, who He is, His glory),

…but **it also speaks of His creation, His glorious design (what He has designed us for).**

It speaks of **a favorable opinion. It has to do with *favor*. It means *to think highly of or to esteem* someone**.

*It has to do with **The Truth (the way it really is, the way God sees it)**.*

*It speaks of what is inherently good and therefore has real glory.*

***It is to be accounted as pleasure. You glory in it. It is to be enjoyed**.*

*It speaks of an estimation of something or someone's true value and worth.*

So, *"The **praise**"* or *"the **glory**"* of men could be seen as:

…the opinion, favor, respect of men that is being enjoyed,

…or it can also actually even be seen as *the very reputation of Man, his value and worth in the flesh,*

…in other words *Man's testimony, Man's experience*

*"The **praise**"* or *"the **glory**"* of God could be seen as:

…the opinion, the TRUTH, the design, the favor, the respect of God,

…and it can even be seen as *the very reputation of God,*

*…what God has to say about Himself and about Man, and what He has to say about Himself in relation to Man, the value and worth He places upon Man because of our original design and true identity in Him, as His offspring and very dear children whom He love.*

These men <u>loved</u> the opinion, the favor, the respect, the very reputation, and value and worth, or *"glory,"* of men **more than** the opinion, more than the TRUTH, more than the design, more than the favor, more than the respect, even more than the very reputation, and value and worth, or *"glory,"* of God, *what God has to say about Man and attach to Man.*

They continued to live in darkness (ignorance, confusion, sin and frustration),

…even though Jesus the Light of the world,

*"…the Light that gives light to every person"*

…had already come into the world!

Can you see that perhaps this is our problem, as well?

**We frustrate the strategy of God, when we shut our ears and our hearts.**

Just like the Jews in Jesus' day would not see what God was trying to say and demonstrate to them in Christ,

*...*we also cannot see what God is trying to say and demonstrate to us in Christ,

*...*because we don't <u>love</u> *The Truth* of God and what it says about us

Instead, we *love* the glory of the flesh.

We *live for* the praise (glory, opinion, favor, value and worth, respect) of men *rather than* the praise (glory, opinion, favor, value and worth, respect) of God.

Proverbs 29:25

*"The fear* (respect, value and worth, favor, opinion, glory) *of Man brings a snare, BUT whoever trusts in the Lord shall be secure* (shall find peace, shall find true satisfaction)*."*

How do you <u>love</u> *The Truth* of God?

By welcoming it, receiving it, embracing it and treasuring it.

By BELIEVING it;

*...*and holding fast to it;

By seeing it for the treasure that it really is;

By being persuaded about it *instead of trying to argue with God over it!*

John 1:14 says that

*"We beheld **His glory** ...full of grace **and truth**."*

So, what is *"**the GLORY**?"*

*...*What is *"**the praise**** (the favorable opinion, the TRUTH, the value and worth, the design, the very reputation) **of God**"*

*...*CONCERNING ***MAN**?*

# *Chapter 10*

## *Crowned with glory & honor*

Hebrews 2:5-9 says this about us,

5 *"For He has not put the world **that was to come**, (the world of **which we live in now**, that is the world) of which we speak..."*

(Notice he is not talking about Heaven one day, the new world, he is talking about this old world God created, planet earth, *this present world we live in after the work of redemption in Jesus Christ has been accomplished*)

*"...He has not placed the world of which we speak..."*

*"...in subjection to angels because..."*

6 *"someone testified in a certain place* (Psalms 8:4-6) *saying:*

**'What is man that You are MINDFUL of him, (that You constantly take thought of him) ...*or the son of man that You* (care so much for and) *TAKE CARE of Him?'***

(In other words, **why is man *so special* to You; of so much *value and worth?*)**

7 *"You have made him a little lower (for a little while lower) than angels…"*

(The original Psalm 8 says: *"than Elohim"* meaning **God Himself**)

*…He confined us for a limited period of time to a fleshly existence, to a lesser dimension than the limitless dimension God enjoys, for only a short season of our existence,*

*NEVERTHELESS*

*"…**You <u>crowned him</u> with <u>glory</u> and <u>honor</u>, and <u>set him over</u> the works of Your hands**,"*

8 *"You have put **<u>all</u> things <u>in subjection</u> under his feet**"*

*"For in that He put **<u>all</u> things <u>in subjection</u> under** him, **He left NOTHING that is not <u>put</u> <u>UNDER him</u>**"*

'*…But now as it is we do not yet see **<u>ALL</u> things put under him**'*

9 *"**BUT WE SEE JESUS**, who for a little while was also made lower than angels,* (restricted to life in a flesh and blood body), ***for the suffering of death,***

(Nevertheless) *CROWNED with GLORY and HONOR, that He, BY THE GRACE OF GOD* (towards US), *might taste death **FOR <u>EVERYONE</u>**."*

So, why is man *worth so much;* so *valuable;* so *important* to God?

He gives us the answer in verse 7.

It is because,

*"You have made him (a little less than) YOURSELF…"*

*"(…and that is why You therefore)* <u>*CROWNED him*</u> *with GLORY and HONOR, and* <u>*SET HIM OVER*</u> *the works of Your hands,"*

Let me tell you something, *God is not embarrassed about mankind. God is not embarrassed about Man's design.*

*HE* made us; *HE* brought us forth *from within Himself* (Gen.1:26, 27), **and thus** *"CROWNED"* <u>us</u> *"with GLORY and HONOR."*

Man is God's personal *representative*, His *companion*, and His *co-ruler*.

We are His very image and likeness!

…being of His being;

…kind of His kind!

…we are His offspring (Acts 17:29).

…we are of the God-kind.

He *"CROWNED"* <u>us</u> to be His co-rulers.

He *"CROWNED"* Man *with His own dominion*.

He made Man *to share His reign and dominion*.

I want you to know, **that *"CROWN"* He gave us is not there for decoration.**

He *"CROWNED"* <u>us</u> *"with GLORY and HONOR,"*

...<u>**to share His reign and dominion**</u>

*"He left <u>NOTHING</u>"* outside of Adam's control;

...**outside of Man's control;**

...**outside of *our* control**

*That's His original plan.*

It's His *one and only plan,*

...**and He has <u>never</u> changed His mind.**

**Man was brought forth out of God**

...*to be God's companion,*

...<u>**nothing less**</u>

I say again:

**_God has companionship with Man in mind,
nothing less._**

Aren't you glad that you are more than a
monkey?

While a monkey, or a dog or a parrot, may
make a good pet, that animal will never be
Man's associate (a companion suitable for
Man).

You see you can train a dog and can draw
some level of friendship and comfort out of that
dog, but you will always remain unfulfilled by it,

...just like it was with Adam, who after he
searched through the whole animal kingdom,
had to admit that he could not find a being in
the same class as him,

...with whom he could truly share equality and
fellowship with,

...someone like himself.

Nothing less, nothing inferior could satisfy.

Do you see the prophetic picture there? How
Adam represented God, being in God's image
and likeness

...how Adam prophetically pointed to God and
represented what was in the heart of God

...I'm talking about before the Fall now?

Can you see that this was a picture in itself, *portraying the desire in the heart of God* **that became His motivation to *make* Man?**

*...to bring Man forth out of His own being?*

...and give us this earth to live in and to richly enjoy?

Listen; **Man is God's kind and God's associate**.

Aren't you glad you are more than dust?

God may have created our bodies from the dust or the clay, but *then He made us out of Himself,*

**He breathed us forth from out of Himself;**

**...out of His LOGOS;**

**...out of His GLORY;**

**...out of His person;**

**...out of His intimate thoughts;**

**...out of His heart;**

**...out of His very being** – Genesis 1:26, 27; 2:7.

God wanted more in Man than just a monkey, or even a parrot that He could teach to talk.

**He wanted a person like unto Himself alone, a spirit-being with a soul, with emotions and personality and a heart, *as His associate and companion in life*.**

Hebrews 2:8

*"For in that He put **all things in subjection under** him, **He left NOTHING that is not put UNDER him**"*

*'Yes, brother Rudi, this all sounds so good, but it is too good to be true; it is too farfetched, it is just lofty words, **my experience prove otherwise**.'*

*'You can just go ahead and ignore that first part of verse 8 you just quoted, brother Rudi, **it doesn't matter what it says**.'*

*'I don't care **what you think it says,** Rudi!'*

*'See, even the writer of Hebrews **agrees with me** ...I mean, just look at what he says right there in the second part of verse 8,'*

*'...But now **as it is** we do not yet see **ALL things under our control**,'*

Friend, please listen to me, ***God's word will never contradict God's heart!***

We can make the Scriptures say just about anything we want it to say, **especially if we want it to agree with our excuses!**

BUT this one thing I have learned, and that is that we can argue with the Scriptures all we want,

…**but if we take the time to read it in context <u>and</u> especially in the light of redemption,**

…**in the light of what we have come to know the heart of God to be,**

…**<u>from what He has revealed about Himself when He took on flesh and blood</u> and became the man Jesus Christ,**

…**in the light of <u>that</u> knowledge of God;**

…**the knowledge of the incarnation;**

…**the knowledge of Redemption,**

…**we are well able to see and understand what the Scriptures really say.**

Hebrews 2:8

*'But now as it is we do not yet see all things under our control.'*

Don't stop there my friend; continue on, read verse 9:

*"BUT WE SEE JESUS…"*

*"CROWNED WITH GLORY AND HONOR"*

*"He by the grace of God tasted death FOR EVERYONE."*

The phrase *"BUT WE SEE JESUS…"* **is not an excuse giver.**

The writer of the book of Hebrews *was not justifying the lame argument against **The Truth*** mentioned in verse 8.

**It is amazing how easily a person can deceive themselves and get caught up in the *"but now as it is"* realities of our own experience,**

*…moaning and groaning about how spiritually week and feeble we are against the strength of sin in our lives.*

We have all these problems, you see, in our experience, and *"we do not yet see **ALL** THINGS"* subject to us,

*…*so we kind of just comfort ourselves and we say; *'but we see Jesus…'*

*'…but **at least** we see Jesus…'*

*…**and so it has become so easy for some to want to see that as a convenient excuse to continue to put up with bondage!***

159

Their whole gospel, you see, those who believe this way, *their whole gospel is a futuristic one,*

*'Maybe one day in Heaven we will reign and be free…'*

*'It is only one day when Jesus comes back that we shall be like Him, brother Rudi!'*

**It is just amazing to me how *they have developed their doctrines to confirm their experience and comfort them in the midst of their problem and lack of victory.***

**When the problem overwhelms them they refer to their doctrine and use it like a tranquilizer, *and feel better about their apparent failure.***

I have but one thing to say to those who think this way:

**Hey listen; *not worrying about it doesn't solve the problem.***

**Ignoring cancer doesn't take it away; *it could kill you if you don't submit to the right treatment to cure it.***

**Making excuses for not dealing with a problem *doesn't solve the problem.***

***And you can't just say that there is no need to worry about it.***

*You can't play with cancer, it will kill you.* **You have got to deal with it <u>aggressively</u>.**

(And notice, for all you people out there, still bound by legalism,

**I did not say** *God will kill you* **for having cancer,**

…**I said** *the cancer will kill you* **if you don't deal with it** *aggressively,* **using the right medicine; submitting to the right treatment, and SIN is the same way.**)

Let me tell you a modern-day parable:

A man went to see a pharmacist about a severe problem in his body, but unfortunately only the assistant of the pharmacist was there and he didn't know enough to help this man.

*So, because of his own self-pride, unwilling to reveal that he didn't know what the right medicine was to cure this man's problem;*

…he just gave the man some tranquilizers and sent him home.

A few days later he again met that man on the street and with a very concerned but nervous and worried look on his face he asked the man concerning his health.

*'Oh,'* the man responded, *'that problem, well, you see, since I took those pills you gave me I*

*feel a little better because of it, and the pain has become somewhat bearable, so I'm just not going to worry about it anymore.'*

Now would you agree with me that that is a very dangerous way to think!

You see tranquilizers and pain medication can make you drowsy, it can make you sleep your life away, *while all the while still dying of cancer.*

**And sad to say, that is exactly what many deceived and ignorant sincere ministers of God have done to us, *they have sold us a bunch of lies and given us religious tranquilizers and painkillers* and now we have spiritually fallen into a religious trance, and we are fast asleep and sleeping our life away!**

Listen to me would you: **That cancer left unchecked will spread through your whole body and destroy the LIFE and STRENGTH you once enjoyed, *and tranquilizers and pain medication is not enough to successfully deal with it and overcome it; it CANNOT,* and it will just drain you even further and aid cancer in sucking the LIFE right out of you.**

**You want to be healed, so you just keep submitting to whatever you're told, *even though it's not really working.***

162

You see, religious people, blindfolded by religion, sincere people, who appear to have a form of godliness; *but who do not really have a handle on the incarnation and the work of redemption,* quite often do not have the answers to life.

You see they have been schooled in the empty religious rituals and traditions and doctrines of men, in cleverly devised little myths and fables,

...oh, they claim to know *"the word of God;" "the word of TRUTH;" "the word of His grace;" "the word of LIFE and TRUTH and LOVE,"*

...but *theirs is another gospel*,

...theirs is a doctrine of demons.

They have really only been schooled in the deceptive doctrines and teachings of men,

...in half-truths and lies disguising themselves as truth

They are confused and don't even realize or know it themselves.

They don't know themselves the keys that make God's kingdom work

**…and all they can give you is just deception, half-truths, and *mere tranquilizers*.**

**Oh, it looks so good;**

***…it appears plausible enough to deal with your guilt,***

***…but it is not enough to cure you.***

These religious men are deceiving us;

*…being deceived themselves!*

*'I am still a sinner and can't seem to overcome it, **but at least I have found a way to deal with my guilt…'***

*'…at least we see Jesus,'*

*'…at least we see His blood shed for our forgiveness.'*

It is just like saying the same thing the spiritually blind and deceived people in John's day was saying;

*'I'm just going to say I have fellowship with God,'*

But just as John did, I would say unto them:

**You can say you have fellowship with God all you want,**

*"BUT WHILE YOU WALK IN DARKNESS* (in ignorance, in confusion, in half-truths, in double-mindedness, in deception and unbelief), *YOU ONLY DECEIVE YOURSELF."*

Hebrews 2:9 starts off with,

*"BUT..."*

That means the writer of Hebrews is answering the argument brought up in verse 8.

He too was not unfamiliar with the age-old argument against *The Truth* that has been around for ages since the fall of Adam ...**to be used as an excuse by every generation when they want to justify their sin**.

You see because, **if we refuse to deal with a sin,** *we must find a way to justify ourselves in putting up with it.*

**It's so convenient to blame it** *on the Fall,*

...**or on God's** *poor design;*

'*...I guess God made me this way. It's just how I am brother!'*

*'I'll pick whatever convenient excuse will work for the moment, just as long as I don't have to admit that the reason I can't overcome is because I am not ready to let go of my sin yet ...whether redemption is a reality; a done deal, or not!'*

The only reason why the writer of Hebrews even brought up the excuse mentioned in verse 8 **is because He wanted to address it head on** *and defeat that argument.*

So, starting verse 9 with a...

## *"**BUT** WE SEE JESUS..."*

...was because He was directly addressing the,

*'But now as it is...'* from verse 8.

He was saying in essence:

**'You may be speaking <u>from your experience</u>, but let me answer your experience with an excuse killer.'**

Hebrews 2:9

## *"**BUT WE SEE JESUS** ...CROWNED WITH GLORY AND HONOR; He by the grace of God tasted death FOR EVERYONE."*

We are so caught up *in our own experience,*

...in the *"as it is"* realities,

...that **we have made more of the Fall of Man than the work of redemption**

**Jesus is the answer to our problem.**

*He is The WAY,*

*...The TRUTH,*

*...and The LIFE!*

**By holding on to our excuses** *we have insulted the work of Grace, and offended Jesus Christ, by whose blood we have been redeemed.*

*"Who gave Himself up for our sins, **that He might deliver us from this present evil age**, according to the will of our God and Father"*
- Galatians 1:4

**Would you dare to believe with me** *what God wants you to believe?*

**Jesus justified the Father's design of the human being,** *and set us free in His work of redemption TO LIVE THAT EXACT DESIGN,*

*...***that's what God wants you to believe!**

I say again:

***Jesus justified the Father's design of Man***

*...***and He also redeemed that design IN US!***

Romans 8:1-4,
1 *"There is therefore now no condemnation **for those who are** (in faith; those who BELIEVE); *those who are in Christ Jesus"*

**(...those who see and understand their inclusion in Christ Jesus; in His work of redemption)**"

Why?

2 *"For the law of* (or the power of) *The Spirit* (the power) *of Life* (*the law of faith;* or the power of God's faith in the work of redemption; **that faith**) *in Christ Jesus* (**my understanding into it and my embracing of it for myself as truth**) *has made me free* from the law of (the power of) *sin and death.*"

3 *"For what the law* (of works; religious do's and don'ts) *could not do* (in other words what Man's own efforts through religion; Man's own religious efforts could not do) *in that it was weak through the flesh,*"

*"For what the Law could not do;* (what religious observance of the Law could not do; what religion itself could not do; what my own religious efforts could not do}, **_God did_ by sending His Son in the likeness of sinful flesh**..."

(God sent Him in a flesh and blood body just like ours, able to be tempted, but He did that,)

*"...on account of sin;* (in other to deal with sin)"
*"He condemned sin"*

(He rendered it powerless over us *by revealing the truth of our original design and true identity;*

168

God being our real Father who genuinely loves us; *"He condemned sin;"* He demonstrated His love to us and thus defeated sin. He put it to shame by defeating it on the cross. *"He condemned sin; He defeated sin"*

"(And thus He stopped its power) *in the flesh,"*

4 *"**so that** the righteous requirement of the law **might be fulfilled in us**..."*

(The end of sin [the end of missing the mark], being dead to sin **and alive to God, caught up in His LOVE; being in love with our Daddy God, living the life of our original design and true identity** *is the righteous requirement of the law*)

"...**so that** the righteous requirement of the law

...**might be fulfilled in us**..."

...**Not by us;**

...**not by our own religious efforts to try and fulfill it,**

**No!**

**He says,**

"...**that the righteous requirement of the law might be fulfilled in us (...by us believing and embracing THE TRUTH)"**

Verse 3 says clearly that,

*"God sent His Son **in the likeness of sinful flesh**"*

**Jesus came *"in the likeness of sinful flesh."***

That means that Jesus came and lived **in the exact same body as ours**;

…that exact same body we blame for all our problems;

…that exact same body the devil wants to claim as his stronghold,

…I mean the very same body the devil, *through emptiness and ignorance and deception causes us to sin in;*

…**Jesus came <u>in that exact same body</u> and *He put sin to shame in it; He defeated it!***

I want you to think about it:

**He lived without sin <u>in that exact same body</u>, even though,**

*"He was tempted in all things just like we are, yet without sin…"*       - Hebrews 4:15

…Simply because *He embraced and knew His true Father;*

170

*…Simply because* He **knew** *and* **believed** *and* **embraced His true identity and authentic original design;**

*…Simply because* He knows and embraces **His True Daddy;**

*…He knew and embraced* His Daddy's **LOVE**

**He proved that these bodies are not able to restrict us from living out our true identity and enjoying it to its full extent;**

**These bodies are not able to restrict us from enjoying the life that God designed us to live,**

…that eternal LIFE, the LIFE of God, that abundant LIFE, *as His very own dear children, whom He loves so deeply,*

*…even in the flesh,*

*…right here on planet earth,*

*…right here in these flesh and blood bodies we can enjoy that kind of life!*

Jesus took away Man's excuse!

He took away our excuse to put up with the devil; *with the father of lies,* in our lives.

If you were to buy a product that continues to break down on you, *wouldn't you be reluctant to buy it again?*

*After a while you will begin to blame the design and point a finger at the designer for making such a poorly designed product.*

In our society today, I am sure you can think of a few things *that have a reputation of being a poorly designed product.*

I have a friend who bought a vehicle designed by Ford, an SUV model. It started acting up almost the first week he bought it, and it proved to be nothing but trouble, lots of trouble. He seemed to run into one problem after another with it, almost on a daily basis, and it caused him great heartache until he finally persuaded the dealer to take it back.

Since then he has met quite a number of other people who also had a similar experience with the same model, and not just with the same model, but with the same Ford brand.

Needless to say, since then he has been very reluctant to ever buy another Ford designed vehicle again, especially an SUV model given its reputation in his eyes.

(Note: Ford has greatly improved their design and manufacturing of their vehicles since then, although many folks are still reluctant to buy into the Ford name again.)

See, in the same way, in Man's mind the question remains, *and it is a question that tends to accuse God;*

*'What is Man, God, that You are MINDFUL of him?'*

I mean,

*'...is God righteous,* **can He justify what He sees in mankind so as to spend all that energy, constantly thinking of him and caring for him?***'*

I mean,

*'...why don't you just wipe mankind out and start all over again, God?'*

I mean,

*'...look at Man, at his history, at his reputation, at the evidence that stands against him as a testimony of his transgression.'*

*'All you have to do is read the local newspaper God!'*

**All this may be true; it may be the testimony of the flesh, *but not the testimony of the Spirit.***

Look at it this way; God *did not* give us a poorly designed model that breaks down every time we try to use it.

**Just because we continue to argue with God over how this product is supposed to be operated,** *and fail to read the manual accurately, or refuse to believe what it actually says,*

*…***does not mean the product doesn't work.**

Romans 3:3 & 4,

3 *"For what if some did not believe?"*

*"Will their unbelief make the faithfulness of God without effect"*

**Will it cancel out God's faith?**

**Can they ever produce enough evidence to cancel out God's Faith?**

4 *"Certainly not!"*

*"Indeed, let God be true but every man a liar."*

*"As it is written: '***You will be justified in Your Words; You will overcome when You are judged.***"*

1John 5:9-11 says,

9 *"If we **receive** (believe and embrace) the witness (the testimony; the experience) of men,"*

*"...the witness* (the testimony; the WORD; THE TRUTH) *of God is greater;"*

*"For this is the witness of God which He has testified of His Son,"*

10 *"that, he who believes in the Son of God has the witness in himself"* (...within his heart;)

*You see, his heart, in agreement with the Holy Spirit, **is bearing strong witness to the truth***

*"...and **he who does not believe God has made Him a liar**,"*

*"...because he has **refused to believe the testimony that God Himself has given** of His Son."*

11 *"And this is the testimony* (God's Testimony)*:"*

***"God has given us eternal LIFE, and this LIFE is in His Son."***

Listen, ***God is not intimidated*** by our experience of failure;

***God is not influenced.***

**He has made up His mind about you and about your design,**

*...and **He is not about to change His mind!***

He knows <u>who you are</u>!

He knows <u>what He has made you to be</u>!

God knows better than to believe the testimony of the flesh,

*...for He designed the human being Himself!*

He knows you are *His offspring;*

...His very image and likeness!

That's why *He likes you,*

...why He is *so attracted to you;*

<u>He knows</u> you are not a failure!

<u>He knows</u> what is *within you;*

...within your capacity to *be!*

You are not a failure;

...you are a *masterpiece*

*...you are a massive success!*

...<u>You are</u> His glory!

God gave us a brand new military F-16 Eagle Fighter Jet. A perfectly designed, precision engineered machine, *well capable of mastering the law of lifts* and soaring high up in the stratosphere;

*…well capable of overriding the law of gravity and drag,* even to the point of breaking the speed of sound several times over;

*…well capable of winning a fight and taking out your enemies!*

**It's not God's fault** if we crash the plane into the ground every time we take off.

Listen; **it really doesn't matter how many times we crash God's plane,**

***…it doesn't change the fact that it is fearfully and wonderfully made!***

***…and well capable of being and doing what it was designed for!***

You see, that scripture in Hebrews 2:9 says:

***"BUT WE SEE JESUS"***

***We see …a new Adam, the original Adam, the authentic original blueprint Son, the One from whom we all came; the One from whom even Adam himself merely derives his design from,***

***"WE SEE HIM; THIS SAME JESUS,"***

***…a new Adam;***

*...the original Adam*

*...introducing a new creation*

*...in His death,*

*...the original re-revealed and now redeemed!*

Everything that Man ever wanted to be, secretly in our hearts;

*...every dream of Man to live a better more glorious life,*

*...a life of true freedom, of irresistible love, of intimate friendship with the living God and with others,*

*...was beautifully displayed in this man Jesus,*

*...and then extended to us in His death.*

You see, everything Man could ever dream to enjoy and to be, *was displayed in Jesus, and thus He justified the Father's design of the human being.*

*So, while we still view Jesus as in a glass case,*

*...as being one of a kind,*

*...doing window-shopping,*

178

*...separating ourselves from His experience*

*...like those Greeks did,*

*...even if they could move Him to do another miracle, they would go home disappointed,*

*...for, that wrong view,*

*...that deception,*

*...<u>would leave them excluded and still frustrated in their own experience</u>.*

Hebrews 2:9

*"**BUT WE SEE JESUS**... **CROWNED** with **GLORY** and **HONOR**..."*

If you consider the account given of Man, *by God,* and then the account of Jesus in Hebrews 2:7 & 9, *you will clearly see that,*

**This Jesus, who was and is and always will be 100% God, willingly laid aside His majesty** (Philippians 2:6-8, John 17:5)

**He was made 100% equal to Adam (to Man's design and being) *for our sake*.**

1Corinthians 15:45

*"The first man Adam became a living being."*

*"The last Adam (Jesus) became a life-giving spirit."*

Jesus is *"the last Adam."*

Not the second Adam,

*"...the last Adam!"*

Jesus became 100% equal to the fallen Adamic race, *for our benefit,*

*...for OUR release from that fallen state!*

History could only record *the death of one man,*

*...but eternity recorded the death of mankind.*

As long as we still judge Jesus *from the wrong point of view,*

*...still just doing window-shopping,*

*...we too will go home disappointed,* like those Greeks.

Hebrews 2:9

*"...He by the grace of God tasted death FOR EVERYONE."*

Paul comes to one conclusion in 2Corinthians 5:14-16,

180

14 *"...We have thus judged* (**concluded**): *that if* (**or since**) *one died for all,_then all died;"*

15 *"and* **He died for all that those who live should live no longer for themselves, but for Him who died for them and rose again."**

16 *"Therefore, from now on,* **we regard NO ONE** (we see no person) *according to* (the testimony of) *the flesh, according to a human point of view* (according to their natural identity) **anymore.**

*...Even though we have even known Christ according to the flesh,* (according to a human point of view; according to His natural identity) *at one point,* **yet now we regard Him thus no longer."**

(...we now know that He represents our salvation, we now know that He is the savior of the world; we now know that He is Savior and Lord; we now know that He was more than just the son of Mary and Joseph; we now know He was and is *the son of God and the son of Man in one body;*

...we now know that He represents our original design;

...we now know that He represents our true identity!

...we now know that He represented the whole human race *in the work of redemption*)

Listen, the only testimony we have had concerning Man is that of men with a fallen experience themselves, living by a belief-system that is flawed, and a viewpoint other than God's,

*...but there is more to Man than we have been taught, if we could only see Man from God's point of view,*

*...it is bound to affect our experience, because our experience is shaped by what we believe about ourselves.*

Proverbs 23:7 clearly states,

*"For as a man **thinks in his heart**, so **is** he."*

Paul said in 1Corinthians 2:2 that he,

*"...wanted to know nothing else among us, except Jesus Christ and Him crucified"*

Paul was determined to continue to see and communicate the value of **every** human being;

*...*what God saw in them; what God designed them for; what God did *to restore them to that original design* in Christ's work of Redemption;

*...*what God did as their Daddy, *to reconcile them, and embrace them in His LOVE!*

Paul was determined to continue to see *every individual* in that light;

…through God's *faith;*

…from God's *point of view;*

…through God's TRUTH and REALITY;

…through God's *knowledge of them;*

…through God's *love and fondness of them!*

He was determined to continue to see and communicate to _every_ person what *God designed them for,*

…and thus what the grace of God _restored them to_ in the death of Christ

2Corinthians 5:16,

16 *"Therefore, from now on, **we regard NO ONE** according to a human point of view* (according to their natural identity) ***anymore."***

According to the apostle Paul,

…*we must consider it part of our ministry* to make known to _all_ mankind *what we were designed for and restored to* in Christ Jesus; *in His incarnation and work of Redemption*

183

According to Paul,

**God <u>entrusted us</u> with *The Word of Truth;***

*...the gospel of <u>Man's salvation</u> in Christ's work of redemption*

Ephesians 3:8 & 9,

8 *"...this grace was given,* **that I (and whomever else gets insight and understanding into it)***"*

*"...this grace was given that I (that* **we all***)*

*...***should preach <u>among the Gentiles</u>** (among the heathen, among the ignorant, among those who still live in sin and for sin; among those who don't know and don't care)

*...that we should preach ...the unsearchable,*

(...not unknowable ...not unreachable, but **inexhaustible**) *riches of Christ,"*

9 *"and* (thus) **to make <u>all people see</u>** *what is* **the fellowship** (what is the intimate knowledge; what is the intimacy produced; what is the encounter enjoyed; what is the LIFE) *of the mystery which from the beginning of the ages has been* **hidden in God***"*

**(...in the heart of God, in the LOGOS of God – the same LOGOS that became flesh and dwelt among us and *is within us.*)**

I want us to continue on this vain of thought for just a little bit longer, **to cement these things in our hearts;**

**...the very things that burned in Paul's heart, and is still burning in God's heart,**

**...to say to us and make known to us!**

The apostle Paul said in Colossians that this was **the focus** of his ministry:

Colossians 1:25-29,

25 *"**God entrusted me with the revelation** (the insight, the understanding) **of this mystery**"*

(...the mystery of our origin, and design, and identity ...and restoration in Christ Jesus;

...the mystery of God being our True Father, *our Daddy, who love us very deeply!*)

*"***God entrusted me with the revelation of this mystery,***

**...so that** *in my ministry to you* **I will make The Word** (this mystery) **known in its full implication.**"*

26 *"**This Word** contained a hidden mystery in past ages and generations"*

*"**BUT it is now revealed** (made fully known) to His saints"*

(...**those who believe it and embrace it and become the products of its persuasion when they hear it;**

...***those who fall in love with the message and with God***)

27 *"To them **God longed** to declare* **(to make fully known)** *the riches **of the glory** of this mystery **on behalf of the nations**"*

**(This thing is for the whole world, not just for a select few of us; believers; Christians; no, everyone is included)**

*"This is the mystery* (This is what we are supposed to make known to all the nations)*:"*

*"**Christ in you**"*

**(In other words we are to make know to the nation that:**

***Christ is in you; His image and likeness is in you; His design is in you; He has been revealed to be in you, indwelling you; being exhibited through you,***

***– Maybe in a very restricted measure because of the ignorance that is in you; because of the influence of deception and of darkness and of the Fall –***

186

BUT nevertheless He is in you, and wants to be exhibited through you.

He wants you to be aware of His presence within you!

He wants to make His abode within you!

He wants to be one with you!)

Our message is:

*Christ in you*

*"Christ in you" fulfills your hope and expectation for glory!*

*"...Christ IN YOU the hope of glory!"*

28 *"Him we preach as we awaken every individual's mind,"*

*"...instructing every individual, bringing them into full enlightenment"*

*"...in order that we may present every person perfect* (mature in understanding and therefore also in expression) *in Christ Jesus."*

29 *"To this end I also labor, consumed with zeal* (an inner drive, motivation, eagerness, passion, the anointing, the zeal of God, the love of God burning in my heart; I am) *infused with His energy* (with His truth and LOVE and

with His very own Spirit) *that **powerfully works within me**.*"

Paul goes on to say there in Galatians 1:15 & 16,

He says:

15 *"God called me into the ministry **through His grace; (through revelation into His grace! Through revelation into what He did in Jesus on my behalf)**;"*

**(God has called me into the ministry by the revelation of His LOGOS to me; His Word; His Truth; His gospel; by the revelation of His incarnation and work of redemption; by His achievement in Christ's death on my behalf)**

16 *"**He separated me from my mother's womb**"*

(He separated me from my natural identity, from the bondage of Man-made religious customs and traditional and futile inaccurate beliefs about myself, and about others, and about God, inherited from my forefathers. *He separated me from all these attachments and references about who I supposedly am*)

16 *"**He separated me from my mother's womb** (from that whole natural identity) **by revealing His Son in me**;"*

*"…**so that I might preach Him** among **and within** the Gentiles…"*

*"The hour has* (now) *come* (has truly come) *that the **son of MAN** should be **glorified**."*
                                                    - John 12:23

But let's return to our discussion in Hebrews 2 quickly.

Hebrews 2:10 & 11

10 *"For it is fitting that He* (God)*, for whom and by whom all things exist, **IN BRINGING** MANY SONS **TO GLORY**,* (It is only logical and appropriate, that, in fulfilling the act of bringing many sons to glory, that God) *should make the pioneer of **THEIR** SALVATION perfect through suffering."*

(Note: Jesus was not made perfect through suffering, He didn't need to be perfected; in Him *the fullness* of the Godhead dwelt in bodily form, **BUT our salvation needed to be perfected,**

Therefore the suffering that is being referred to is the *"suffering of death"* mentioned in verse 9 that made His sacrifice and therefore our redemption perfect.)

11 *"For He* (Jesus) *who sanctifies* (through His suffering of death) *and those* (us) *who are sanctified* (through that exact same sacrifice of Jesus)"*

189

*"...HAVE ALL ONE ORIGIN."*

*"That is why HE IS NOT ASHAMED TO CALL THEM (US) <u>BRETHREN</u>,"*

Did you catch that?

He says,

*"We have all one origin!"*

**We all have the same origin,**

**...the same Father,**

**...both Jesus and us!**

*...we originated from the same source,*

*...we share the same mold!*

*...the same identity!*

*...the same image and likeness!*

*...the same nature!*

*...we are partakers of the Divine nature!*

*...it is within us already!*

*...we may not be drawing from it like He did, but it is within us none the less!*

In John 12 Jesus said about His death that,

*"Now is the time for the **son of MAN** to be **GLORIFIED**"*

...and so here in Hebrews 2:10 we read that he became,

*"...the **PIONEER**"* (the FIRST one of many BRETHREN)*"*

He is *"the **PIONEER** ...IN BRINGING MANY SONS TO <u>GLORY</u>."*

**Listen, God had nothing less in mind <u>for us</u> *than what He was able to display in Jesus.***

Verse 11 says that,

*"<u>WE</u>* (Jesus and us) *are of the same origin,"*

...**of the same substance!**

*He is our blueprint and God is our Father.*

**Father God is not just Jesus' Father;**

*...He is <u>our</u> Father.*

*He is our Source;*

*...we come from Him.*

*He is our Daddy!*

*Father God is our Daddy ...and Jesus is our blueprint!*

191

He (Jesus) is *"the **PIONEER;" (the preeminent One**)"*

…some translations say,

*"…the **author,"***

*"…of **THEIR** SALVATION…"*

Who's *"SALVATION?"*

**OURS**!!!

**God displayed nothing more in Jesus *than He was able to restore and release US into;***

**…through HIS FAITH *AND NOW OUR FAITH* in the salvation Jesus bought FOR US with His blood.**

I want you to know that **God doesn't plan and fail.**

*Exactly what He had in mind from the beginning is what we are restored to.*

In Hebrews 2:10 we see that **it is His suffering that brought US glory**

…and **therefore** in verse 11 it is written that,

*"HE IS NOT ASHAMED TO CALL **US** BRETHREN."*

**What He had in mind for us is nothing less**

***…than SONSHIP of equal standing with Jesus!***

For to this 1Corinthians 1:9 also bears strong witness, which says,

*"God… has called us into <u>the</u> fellowship <u>of</u> His Son"*

**It is nothing inferior, nothing less;**

**…it is not an inferior fellowship,**

**…it is the exact same fellowship**

Also Romans 8:29 says,

*"God jointly formed us <u>in the image of His Son</u>,"*

*"…so that He might be <u>the first born among many brethren</u>."*

**(He pre-planned for us to be restored in that exact image of His Son, in His death and resurrection; *so that He might be the first born among many brethren*)**

In the light of all this I remind you again of what Jesus said in John 12:36

*"While you have the light, <u>believe in the light</u>, (embrace the light; absorb the light), <u>so that you might become light</u>."*

194

# Chapter 11

## Taking up Arms

Peter reveals to us how His suffering had EVERYTHING to do with OUR GLORY; **with our GLORIFICATION,** he says:

1Peter 2:24

*"Who Himself bore **OUR** sins in His own body on the tree, so that **WE**, HAVING DIED (past tense) TO SINS…"*

So, when did <u>we</u> die to sin?

**In the death of Jesus!**

*"…so that **WE, <u>HAVING DIED</u>** TO SINS, might **LIVE in righteousness** – by whose stripes **WE WERE** HEAL<u>ED</u> (past tense)."*

Note: **We also now have a LEGAL RIGHT in the spirit to be healed physically as well.**

**Whose sins did He die for?**

*"…**OUR** sins!"*

**But as long as you <u>still</u> just see Jesus,**

*...and not yourself included in His death, burial, resurrection and ascension; in His work of redemption,*

...as long as you <u>just see Jesus</u>,

...you will continue to think of Him as the Son of God, who lived a wonderful life and died a sad death,

*...and you will sentimentally celebrate that event in history,*

...as just another religious festival, perhaps in your mind the greatest of all, *but still just a sentimental religious event!*

Listen; there is nothing the devil desires more than <u>to keep *mankind* ignorant</u> of the LEGAL AND VERY VITAL IMPLICATIONS of the sufferings of Jesus.

BUT,

*"He Himself took <u>OUR</u> sin, <u>THAT WE</u> (in that one act; in that one event) <u>MIGHT DIE TO SIN</u> and LIVE to righteousness."*

HOW DO YOU DIE TO SIN?

By *<u>FAITH</u> in that one event;*

*...by <u>faith</u> in that one act of His <u>that released you</u>!*

Romans 6:5 says,

*"**SEEING THEN**, that **WE** **ARE** united with Him in death,"*

Romans 6:11 says,

*"**CONSIDER** YOURSELVES **THEREFORE**…"*

(In other words: *Come to an accurate mathematical **conclusion**, based on a correct* evaluation of all the facts, and logical deductive reasoning, *which brings persuasion and conviction*)

*"**CONSIDER** **YOURSELVES** (**THEREFORE**) dead unto sin."*

1 Peter 4:1 says,

*"THEREFORE, **SEEING THAT** Christ suffered FOR **US** in the flesh, **ARM** YOURSELVES also with THE SAME MIND* (or with **the same understanding;** with **the same persuasion**)*"*

*"FOR he* (meaning YOU) *who **HAS*** (past tense) *suffered in the flesh…"*

When did I suffer in the flesh?

**IN** **HIS** **DEATH!**

*"FOR he* (meaning YOU) *who **HAS*** (past tense) *suffered in the flesh …**HAS** ceased from sin."*

This Scripture tells us exactly how to appropriate the <u>LEGAL</u> IMPLICATIONS of His obedience,

*...BUT, it is not through <u>casually agreeing</u> with God,* I can tell you that much!

You don't overcome the devil by casually resisting him; *in the same way you can't overcome a thief on your property by casually resisting him.*

No, let me tell you, YOU APPROPRIATE THE LEGAL IMPLICATIONS OF JESUS' OBEDIENCE BY COMING INTO *AGGRESSIVE AGREEMENT* WITH GOD,

*...<u>BEING TOTALLY PURSUEADED IN HIS TRUTH</u>.*

The ONLY way to take up arms for warfare is AGRESSIVELY!

To make a casual stand against the enemy is <u>SURE</u> DEFEAT!

2Corinthians 10:3-5 tells us that

*"The weapons THAT WE HAVE to stand our ground against the devil ARE <u>MIGHTY</u>,* (NOT WEAK, but *"<u>MIGHTY</u>"), to pull down STRONGHOLDS..."*

Okay now, before you think you have to go to war with the devil, *remember that Jesus already defeated Him.*

So you are not really engaging the devil *in a fight.*

Where are these *"STRONGHOLDS"* located *that you are supposed to tear down?*

**In the *"VAIN IMAGINATIONS"* of THE MIND!**

These are thoughts that come from THE MINDSET of this world; **an un-enlightened mind, a mind ruled by darkness,**

**...a mind ruled by ignorance, confusion, double-mindedness, *half-truths, lies and deception*.**

**I want you to know that THE MINDSET of the world is a THOUGHT-PROCESS,**

**...based on the futile *inaccurate misguided traditions and beliefs* of their forefathers,**

**...*inspired by Man's experience as a fallen creature!***

**It is a THOUGHT-PROCESS, a BELIEF-SYSTEM,**

**...heavily influenced and inspired by the devil; *the father of lies and illusions himself.***

You can go study the following Scriptures for yourself and see what the Bible has to say about this, [1John 5:19, 2Corintians 4:3,4],

...and I am sure there are many more you can find on your own that says the same thing.

You see, **if we don't live by God's viewpoint,** those THOUGHTS *inspired by Man's experience as a fallen creature,* those THOUGHTS *based on the futile inaccurate and misguided traditions, beliefs, teaching and doctrines of our forefathers* BECOME *"STRONGHOLDS,"*

**...a landing strip for the enemy, so he can gain entrance into your life, at any time,** *from the outside in,* **whenever he so desires.**

These THINKING-PATERNS, these *"STRONGHOLDS"* OF THOUGHT **begin to** *feed* **lust, fear, and anger and so on.**

Satan knows how to exploit these *"STRONGHOLDS"* OF THOUGHT *in his effort to introduce deception and spoil* ***your understanding of THE TRUTH,***

...and so to spoil, *in your conscience,* your standing before God, and to spoil *your witness before other people,*

...but I praise God, that, **God's truth is so <u>much stronger</u> than the devil's deceptions**.

God declares in the scriptures that,

*"...the weapons HE GAVE US to chase the devil off with, are <u>MIGHTY</u>, not weak."*

He tells us *"to ARM <u>OURSELVES</u>"* with these *weapons;*

*...*with these *thoughts;* with these *truths;* with these *redemption conclusions;*

*...to arm ourselves with these things,* against the enemy

That is exactly what these weapons are, what *"THE SWORD OF THE SPIRIT"* is:

It is the Truth of God; the understanding given to us from the Scriptures; *in Jesus; in the LOGOS; in the WORD made flesh.*

What God has revealed in Him is the keys to freedom.

These insights, which open God's kingdom within us;

*...*which open (righteousness, peace and joy) to us *and causes it to work in our lives* is the very *"weapons of our warfare;"*

*...*it is *"THE SWORD of the Spirit"* by which we arm ourselves and arm our minds to resist our enemy and stand fast against our enemy and overcome!

Jesus said Himself, in John 8:32:

*"You shall **KNOW** (In the Greek: EPICNOSCO: to have revelation, insight and understanding into, **to fully know**)"*

*"You shall **KNOW THE TRUTH**, and (then that insight into it; that **persuasion** in) THE TRUTH shall make you free."*

2Corinthians 10:5 continues, It says:

*"...bringing INTO CAPTIVITY **EVERY THOUGHT** that exalts itself against THE KNOWLEDGE of God..."*

*"...bringing INTO CAPTIVITY EVERY THOUGHT ...to **THE OBEDIENCE OF CHRIST**"*

What does it mean to take *"**EVERY THOUGHT**"* captive?

In the original Greek language it literally means: **TO ARREST** AT SPEARPOINT.

I also want you to notice that this verse says:

*"THE OBEDIENCE **OF** CHRIST,"*

**In other words, *knowing and believing* what His obedience to the Father LEGALLY made available TO US *is our weapon of defense,***

...*knowing* that our enemy has no more LEGAL right to reign over us with anything,

...*knowing the success and truth of redemption and restoration of who we are; our original design and true identity; our very relationship as God's own dear children,*

...*knowing* these things; *these TRUTHS,* we can resist him (the father of lies),

"...*steadfast in THE FAITH,*"

...with *full knowledge;*

...*full conviction,*

...and with *full authority* in our lives!

We are to,

"...bring INTO CAPTIVITY **EVERY THOUGHT**,"

...to *"THE KNOWLEDGE,"*

...to the full knowledge of;

...to the very,

*"OBEDIENCE OF CHRIST JESUS"*

Can you now see how *"THE KNOWLEDGE,"* the *full knowledge* of THE TRUTH revealed and testified to in the Scriptures *become our victory!*

Jesus Himself overcame the devil by His knowledge; *by His insight and understanding into the Scriptures and the LOGOS of God;* **the very thoughts of God; the truth of God; God's reality!**

He overcame the devil with the *"word of TRUTH,"* when He said:

*"Satan **it is written!**"*

There is absolutely nothing quite as piercing and as deeply penetrating *as the LOGOS;* **as the TRUTH OF GOD!**

Hebrews 4:12 states,

*"For the word of God is living and powerful, and sharper than any two-edged sword* (or spear point for that matter)*, piercing even to the division of soul and spirit, and of joints and marrow,* **and is a discerner of the THOUGHTS and INTENTS OF THE HEART.**"

**Can you see how** *"the Word of TRUTH"* **deals with the natural minded THOUGHTS and BELIEFS based on Man's OPINIONS; based on Man's EXPERIENCE as a fallen creature** *...under the influence and manipulation and dominion of the father of LIES and DECEPTION!*

**Listen, the truth revealed in Jesus is your victory over the world and the devil,**

**...so <u>ARM</u> YOUR OWN MIND, to confront and overcome ANY size contradiction with YOUR PERSUASION;**

**...with your conviction in *"the word of TRUTH."***

1John 5:4

*"...this is the victory that overcomes the world, **even our FAITH**"*

**The devil's whole strategy is to question the <u>GLORY</u> restored to you?**

If the consequence of Jesus' death is **OUR GLORY,**

...then it is only logical that Satan's whole strategy would be *to belittle you, **to make you less than,***

*...at least in your mind;*

***...to make you less than God says of you in His opinion (His TRUTH) of you!***

Satan wins his greatest victory **if he can paralyze you and neutralize you, and fill you with inability,**

**...by loading your mind with guilt and inferiority,** *and you RECEIVE that into your spirit.*

If he can hold you captive under an OLD identity; a false identity; lies and deception; under *"STRONGHOLDS"* of fleshly (natural, Man-made) judgments, based on Man's opinions as a fallen creature; the witness of Man, not God's,

*...then he can frustrate THE PLAN OF GOD, the strategy of God* **to reproduce His glory in YOU; in YOUR flesh; in YOUR natural body,** *in order to reach your neighbor and ultimately the world.*

**Can you see how putting up with** *sin;* **with** *lies* **and** *deception, would seek to interrupt the manifestation of glory, the experience of glory?*

*...***It would seek to interrupt** *your testimony*;

*...***it would seek to interrupt** *God's desire* **to fill the earth with the knowledge of His glory,** *to reveal His design* **for every human being,** *through YOUR life, and in YOUR experience!*

BUT now Peter adds his five cents and He says in 1Peter 4:1, *'Hey listen man!'*

*"...since Christ suffered FOR US in the flesh,* **ARM <u>YOURSELVES</u>** *ALSO* **WITH <u>THIS</u> MIND,**

*for he who **has** suffer**ed** in the flesh **has** ceas**ed** from sin"*

**We don't have to suffer again in the flesh to get free from sin,**

*...**no, Christ suffered for us in the flesh,***

*...***SO THAT WE SHOULD, AND COULD, AND WOULD**, CEASE FROM SIN.*

In chapter 2:24 Peter continues, He says,

1Peter 2:24

*"He Himself bore OUR sins in His own body on the tree, that **WE, HAVING DIED** TO SINS, **MIGHT** (by FAITH; by **revelation**; be FREE to) **LIVE** IN RIGHTEOUSNESS"*

**That we might live in the understanding of THE TRUTH;**

**...live enjoying abundant LIFE;**

**...live FREE in the FREEDOM IN WHICH CHRIST HAS SET US FREE;**

**...live enjoying intimate friendship with the living miracle working God,**

**...OUR VERY OWN PAPA;**

**...OUR DADDY; OUR TRUE FATHER!**

That's why he also says in 1Peter 4:2,

*"**WE NO LONGER** should live, **THE REST OF OUR TIME IN THE FLESH** for the lusts of men* (for <u>the strong desires of men</u>, *that are nothing but the fruit of their deception*)*"*

*"...**We should no longer live the rest of our time in the flesh for these things**, but for the will of God."*

When?

One day in Heaven only?

**NO!**

He says,

*"...**THE REST OF OUR TIME <u>IN THIS FLESH BODY</u>!!!!**"*

People are so quick to want to use that Scripture that says that *"all have sinned and fallen short of glory"* as an excuse for their failure,

...but they seem to be ignorant of the fact that those who have received the *"word of truth,"*

...those who have **believed it and embraced it**,

...those who are born of *faith*,

208

…recognizing that they are *born from above*,

…they *are indeed new creations!*

People are so quick *to excuse **their own
failure***, at the expense of the IN-YOUR-FACE
fact that the glory Man fell from ***has been
restored to them <u>already COMPLETELY</u>*** *"in
the resurrection of Jesus Christ from the dead,"*

…and that ***they have been <u>already
COMPLETELY</u>*** *"justified **freely** by His grace
**through the redemption** that is in Christ
Jesus"*

Listen, my friend, **YOUR FREEDOM** *in which
Christ Jesus* **HAS SET YOU FREE** *is at stake
here!*

I know this is strong language and I know I am
belaboring the point, *but I am trying to get you
to think, I am trying to reason with you and
persuade you, and get you to thoroughly
understand that **God had a specific design in
mind for Man,***

…just like I believe the man had who works for
Ford Motor Company, and designed my
friend's SUV model vehicle.

Now if this man, and Ford Motor Company, put
it on the market for the first time, and got lots of
complaints like, *'This product doesn't live up to
its glossy advertisement,'* or,

*'What you said about how it was going to work doesn't match our experience, it just doesn't line up with it; it falls apart every time we switch it on!'*

*'It just doesn't work, sir, what you have said, legally, positionally, doesn't line up with the experiential, the practical!'*

Do you think that that man, or Ford Motor Company, *would be able to have confidence in their product* after that?

Neither the Ford Motor Company, nor the man who designed the vehicle, *nor God Himself, for that matter* **concerning _our_ design,** would have any further confidence whatsoever to market His product; **us;** to market **His design of us** again,

*...**unless** He already has a proven flawless design, unless He already has a prototype with a flawless track record,*

**Jesus is that prototype!**

**In Jesus, God carries around the guarantee that gives Him enough confidence in His own heart;**

*...He has the guarantee of a successful display of the life He designed, and desires for Man to live, in His Son's 33 years on earth.*

Jesus fully displayed that LIFE successfully,

...and then was cut off,

...*so WE COULD BE grafted in THROUGH FAITH.*

He left us with no excuse.

If we now fail at it, *it is simply because we fail to renew our minds with a proper understanding of what we were designed for,*

...it is <u>because we fail to appropriate</u> the *"word of Truth,"* in our lives!

We fail at being who we were designed to be, *because we fail to BELIEVE it;*

...*because we prefer an alternative to the TRUTH;*

...*because we prefer an assumed false identity,*

...because we prefer darkness over light; we prefer our own *self-deception.*

We fail, and give into the lie and deception, because we fail to STAND FIRM IN THE TRUTH and *<u>aggressively</u>* resist the devil,

...for if we did, <u>standing *steadfast* and *immovable*</u> in THE FAITH, (in the understanding and persuasion of THE TRUTH), *he would be forced to flee from us,* amen!

Jesus was fully able to live His life in this body, *this selfsame body we blame for all our problems, this selfsame body we constantly, conveniently accuse of being flawed,*

...He lived His life in it, *without being intimidated by it; without seeing it as weak and inferior and a challenge to live in.*

The same LOGOS; the same WORD; *the same life designed for us from the beginning,* became RHEMA, it became flesh in Jesus Christ.

There is nothing wrong with our design!

We have no right to use it as an excuse and so INSULT Him who designed it from the beginning *for His glory to be revealed and manifested in it and through it!*

Colossians 2:9 & 10 declares,

*"For in Him* (in Jesus) *dwells all the fullness of the Godhead* **BODILY***;*

*...AND <u>YOUR COMPLETENESS IS ON DISPLAY</u> in Him."*

Your completeness was revealed and restored in Him!

*"You are complete in Him!"*

There is nothing weak about your redemption!

There is nothing weak in God's ability to restore you to the place He prepared for you in Christ Jesus, *and are able to release you into, and uphold you in, through Truth and through Faith.*

By FAITH'S EMBRACE we enter into these things;

By FAITH we are restored and released into the salvation Jesus bought for us.

That FAITH is not of ourselves; *it is birthed in us.*

*...it is a gift from God* that comes to us when GOD'S TRUTH *becomes clear to us.*

*"By GRACE,* [through what the Father did for us in Jesus], *are you saved, THROUGH FAITH, and that not of yourselves, it is the gift of God"* – Ephesians 2:8

You see, **God's FAITH in the salvation Jesus bought with His blood is where we draw FAITH from.**

213

God first believed in that salvation, and that's what has given us permission to believe it *and be persuaded in it* as well.

It was God's FAITH that restored and released us into that salvation.

We enter in by FAITH, but it is God's FAITH that restored and released us into that salvation.

OUR FAITH is merely inspired by HIS FAITH.

1Corinthians 2:7

*"But we speak the wisdom of God in a mystery, the hidden wisdom which **GOD ORDIANED** EVEN BEFORE THE AGES, **FOR OUR GLORIFICATION**."*

When God speaks *it is as good as done,* and He Himself *ordained* our glory.

When God promises or decrees, or says something, *His own being is behind it,* and it will be exactly as He has said.

We are talking about the revealed plan and purpose of God for Man.

Verse 8 goes on to say, talking about the wisdom of God; talking about the mystery; about God ordaining us for glory; about our glorification, it says:

1Corinthians 2:8

*"...which none of the rulers of this age knew,*

(*...which none of them grasped or understood or even had a clue about. He is talking about the devil and his imps, not just the religious and political governing authorities, none of them knew about this, it was a hidden mystery; **it was hidden from them**)"*

*"...for had they known they would not have crucified THE LORD **OF GLORY**."*

I want us to really see this clearly!

What exactly was this secret Paul was talking about;

...what was the hidden plan of God?

...what was the information hidden to the enemy that would have so influenced his conduct that he would not have crucified Jesus had he known the content of that secret?

That secret; that hidden plan of God was hidden from the enemy's sight, *so he could not interrupt the plan of God;*

...***but thank God it was not hidden from us,***

*...only from the devil!*

Paul says in verse 7:

*"…**WE** SPEAK the wisdom of God concerning this mystery…"*

…and in verse 10 he says,

*"But God **HAS REVEALED** IT **TO US** through the Spirit."*

So, this mystery is not hidden *from the world, **from us.***

**WE CAN KNOW** this mystery.

It was hidden FOR OUR SAKES from the devil.

**God didn't want to *keep it hidden from US;* He wants US to know!**

**Ignorance is the tool of the devil, not God's.**

God's desire is to **MAKE KNOWN** TO US **what has been hidden in His heart from the very beginning.**

**He does not desire to remain some mysterious person.**

**He wants US to KNOW what HIS PLANS and THOUGHTS are;**

*…***what His HEART is TOWARDS US!**

This is the mystery hidden from the devil:

216

If he knew that THE DEATH OF JESUS WOULD BE THAT CORN OF WHEAT Jesus talked about in John 12:24, *that falls into the earth and PRODUCE MANY MORE AFTER ITS OWN KIND,* then he would never have done it.

John 12:24 is what Jesus said in response to hearing about those Greeks wanting to see Him;

*"MOST ASSUREDLY, I say unto you, unless a grain of wheat falls into the ground and dies it remains alone, but if it dies, IT PRODUCES MUCH GRAIN."*

See, the devil thought that it was the end of the corn of wheat when he buried it, *he thought he was rid of it for good,*

...BUT IN THE LIFE OF THAT ONE CORN *WAS HIDDEN A HARVEST* THAT WOULD FLOOD AND FILL THE EARTH.

Hallelujah!!!!

If you will dare to begin to focus on and *AGRESSIVELY BELIEVE* that the life of Jesus is THE REVELATION of YOUR TRUE DESIGN,

...you will not only be able to successfully frustrate the strategy of the evil one in your own life,

**...BUT GOD WILL HAVE HIS HARVEST THROUGH YOU!!!!**

I believe that is exactly what Jesus said in John 12:36,

*"While you have the light,* **BELIEVE IN THE LIGHT***,* **that** **_YOU_** *MIGHT BECOME* **SONS OF THE LIGHT***."*

**"...that you might become products of the light; carriers of the light;"**

**...carrying forth the light into the darkness that covers the face of the earth;**

**...you will obliterate the deep darkness covering the people!**

# Chapter 12

## You Already Qualify

There is nothing the devil can do to reverse what God has done.

It means that there is no weapon that he can form; no fiery dart he can successfully throw at you that could disqualify you.

**GOD QUALIFIED YOU, amen!**

Colossians 1:12 says so!

*"...giving thanks to* **THE FATHER WHO QUALIFIED US***..."*

*"...***to be partakers of this inheritance (GIVEN TO US)** *in* **the light***."*

The masses are seeking what we have, what I have and hopefully, *what you now also have, through this book.*

*The masses are seeking true fulfillment;* they are seeking to be qualified for glory.

God *has already qualified them in Christ Jesus* for His glory, for His positive recognition.

He has *already qualified them for a new identity.*

He has qualified them to be restored, *through the birth of faith in their hearts,* to be restored, to their original design; to their true identity; to their Daddy God; to their true Father who loves them.

So don't just intellectualize about it, *and enjoy it secretly for yourself, and revel in it in private, go do something with it,*

GO TELL SOMEONE THE GOOD NEWS!

*Stop disqualifying them by looking at them from a natural point of view*

*…prejudging them according to their natural identity, or their mindset, or their behavior;*

*…you never REALLY know how someone will respond,*

*…or who will respond positively to this good news!*

*Their hearts were designed for the TRUTH!*

*Don't look at their countenance or their surface response;*

...be assured that the Holy Spirit, *in agreement with their own hearts,* **will bear strong witness within them to this gospel.**

**God wants to win their hearts forever *with this good _news_!***

...and IT IS *GOOD* <u>NEWS</u>!!!

Hallelujah!

**IT IS THE BEST *<u>NEWS</u>*.**

IT IS EXCEEDINGLY ABUNDANTLY ABOVE AND BEYOND *WHAT THEY COULD EVER HAVE HOPED OR DREAMED!!!!*

Please turn with me in your Bible to 2Corinthians 4:6-11, and 3:18. *I want to show you something you will really enjoy:*

2Corinthians 4:6 says

6 *"For **IT IS THE GOD who command light to shine out of darkness who <u>HAS SHONE INTO OUR HEARTS</u>"***

*"...**to give THE LIGHT (THE UNDERSTANDING; THE ACCURATE TRUTH) OF <u>THE KNOWLEDGE</u>...**"*

What knowledge is that?

*"...THE KNOWLEDGE ...of the GLORY of God in the face of Christ Jesus ...who is the image of God"*

**That KNOWLEDGE; that ACCURATE TRUTH; that GLORY has to do with <u>the IMAGE OF GOD</u>***... the very image we were originally made in!*

*"...the GLORY of God* **(the very image and likeness of God,** on display in Jesus) *in the face of Christ Jesus"*

...is ***"THE VERY KNOWLEDGE"*** **of who God is and of who we truly are;**

...it is the LOGOS on display; *"THE WORD made flesh;"* it is the LIGHT OF GOD; the TRUTH OF GOD,

*...the very Spirit and heart and true image of the living God,*

*...the image and likeness in which we were made!*

**That is what was** *revealed* **in Christ Jesus**

7 *"BUT WE HAVE* ***THIS TREASURE*** (The knowledge of God made known; the LOGOS of God revealed; the GLORY of God on display; *the very image and likeness of God restored*) *in earthen vessels* (in flesh and blood bodies),

(…we have the very Spirit and heart and true image of the living God; *that very Spirit of the Living God himself,* ALIVE IN US,)

"…**that the excellence of the power,** (the power to be what we were designed to be; the power to change people's lives)*, **may be OF GOD**, (and not merely from us)*"

This TREASURE, this GOOD *NEWS*, this TRUTH, *of us being restored completely to the image and likeness of God; to God's Spirit; to God Himself,* **is not just some cleverly devised Man-made myth, fable or theory we thought up by ourselves, NO!**

*IT IS OF GOD!*

**VISIBLE IN JESUS was and is the DOXA;**

*…the very GLORY;* **THE OPINION; THE TRUTH; THE POSITIVE RECOGNITION OF GOD,**

*…CONCERNING MAN'S DESIGN,*

*…THE VERY IMAGE AND LIKENESS OF THE INVISIBLE GOD, THE VERY SPIRIT OF THE LIVING GOD, THAT VERY NATURE OF GOD WE WERE DESIGNED FOR*

*…WAS MADE VISIBLE IN JESUS!*

*…and then RESTORED TO US!*

We have, *through the birth of faith in our hearts;* we have *THIS TREASURE* in earthen vessels,

And notice; THE TREASURE is not intimidated *or somehow limited* by the earthen vessel.

The GLORY of the treasure *remains INTACT,*

...in fact, *the treasure AFFECTS the vessel,* not the other way around;

...*the vessel takes ITS VALUE from the treasure it holds!*

2Corinthians 3:18 says,

"But *WE ALL* (**NOW**, after the work of redemption; after what has been revealed in Christ Jesus, *WE ALL*)

...*with unveiled face,* (...that means it is not hidden but revealed; we are no longer ignorant of it, because *WE ALL*)

...*ARE BEHOLDING AS IN A MIRROR*

...*THE GLORY OF THE LORD,"*

So, as we are looking intently at THE GLORY OF THE LORD;

...*at the work of redemption;*

...at THE TRUTH of **our original design** and **true identity,**

...**as it is revealed in Jesus;**

...*we are seeing the glory* **we fell from,**

...we are *seeing* **the very image and likeness of God,**

...*in which we have been made,*

...we are *seeing* the very Spirit of the invisible God **on display;**

...*that Divine Nature* ***we were designed for,***

...we are *seeing* THAT GLORY ***redeemed and restored;***

...*we are seeing **THAT GLORY** <u>in us</u>,*

...<u>***STILL INTACT IN SPITE OF THE FALL***</u>

...*it is* ***the GLORY*** *of the Lord;*

...***His image; His likeness; His Divine Nature; His LOVE,***

...<u>***in us already***</u>*!*

*We are discovering <u>what is in us</u>.*

**It is the same as if we were looking into *A MIRROR*.**

**What do you *see reflected* when you look at *a mirror?***

*You see your own true reflection there!*

*You see YOURSELF;*

*…your TRUE face <u>REVEALED</u>!*

*THE MIRROR DOESN'T LIE*

*It accurately reveals YOU;*

*…the <u>REAL YOU</u>!*

*…Not the <u>POTENTIAL</u> you!*

*…IT ACCURATELY REVEALS <u>THE REAL YOU</u>!*)

2Corinthians 3:18,

*"…BEHOLDING <u>AS IN A MIRROR</u> THE GLORY OF THE LORD,"*

*…and* **(as we BEHOLD it; as we encounter that REALITY)** *WE ARE <u>INSTANTLY</u>*

*"…TRANSFORMED INTO <u>THE VERY SAME IMAGE</u>"*

*"…WE ARE INSTANTLY TRANSFORMED"*

*…by REVELATION;*

226

*...**by REALIZING THE TRUTH;***

Why?

Because **we ARE *children of God,***

Because it is ***our image*** we see there;

*...**our original design; our true identity,***
— Genesis 1:26, 27

*"...we are beholding **as in a mirror** the glory of the Lord, and we are changed* (instantly)*; we are transformed* (in our believing and in our thinking and in our outward expression) ***into the same image*** (we see in that mirror)*, **from glory to glory**,"*

*...from the fading glory of the flesh;*

*...from the inferior glory of our natural inferior identity, **to His glory;***

*...the glory **of our true identity and design,***

*"...**by the Spirit of the Lord**"*

*...**by the TRUTH;***

*...**by the SPIRIT OF TRUTH HIMSELF**;*

*...**by REALITY revealed WITHIN US; within our inner-man; within our spirit-man, to us,***

*...**by the Spirit of the Lord!***

*His living Holy Spirit; the Spirit of Truth* **is bearing** *strong witness* **in our hearts,**

*…and He brings faith* **into our hearts,**

*…<u>and as we yield to His Spirit, and to that faith</u>,*

*…*we are instantly transformed *<u>by that faith,</u>*

*…<u>and by the power of the Holy Spirit</u>*

*…*into that very image *we now SEE;*

*…*that image *which is <u>already inside of us</u>.*

You see; it is the glory of God *revealed in Jesus* <u>that becomes the mirror of our lives</u>,

*…because of what was revealed in His incarnation,*

*…and because of what was accomplished in His sufferings on our behalf.*

We <u>see</u> OURSELVES there!

We <u>see</u> what is ALREADY WITHIN US there!

*…there …in the incarnation, and in the work of redemption!*

If we are still doing *window shopping;* if we are still seeing Jesus as in *a glass case,* **instead of** *seeing Him <u>as a mirror</u>;*

*...*Instead of *SEEING,*

*...*that <u>He RESTORED US to</u> *the same* image and likeness, the same *quality of life* before the Father,

*...that same quality of intimate friendship* with the Father, *that He Himself enjoys,*

*...*if we don't *see THAT,*

*...*then we will continue to strive to attain to His standard of living, through religion, through legalism; through religious do's and don'ts; through works;

*...through our own misguided efforts at self-improvement!*

Next time you read 1Corinthians 13,

*...*begin to *realize* that *it is <u>your LIFE</u>* on display there;

*...<u>it is</u> whom you are now FREE <u>to be</u>;*

*...*not something you need to *strive to live up to,*

*...*or someone you need to *try and become.*

Stop doing window-shopping,

*...*and *start looking into the <u>mirror</u>,*

...discovering *who you are;*

...discovering <u>what is yours already</u>,

...*because of <u>who you are</u>* in Christ,

...*because of what <u>He HAS REVEALED</u> about you!*

1Corinthians 2:12 says,

*"**NOW WE HAVE RECEIVED**, not the spirit of this world, but the Spirit who is from God, **THAT WE MIGHT KNOW <u>THE THINGS</u> THAT <u>HAVE BEEN</u> FREELY GIVEN <u>TO US</u> <u>BY</u> <u>GOD</u>."***

**If we want to live, *enjoying an experience that confirms these things,***

**Then it is important for us *to really understand* 1John 5:9:**

*"If we receive the witness;* (the testimony, the opinion, the thought-process, the belief-system), *of men,"*

*"...**THE WITNESS;** (the **TESTIMONY**, the **OPINION**, the **TRUTH** and the **FAITH**) **<u>OF</u> <u>GOD</u> <u>IS</u> <u>MUCH</u> <u>GREATOR</u>;"***

*"...**for this is THE WITNESS** (the **FAITH**) *of God that He has testified of His Son:"***

*"…**God has given us ETERNAL LIFE**
(ETERNAL TRUTH; that LIFE that was from
the beginning), **and this life** (this spirit-life; that
eternal truth) **is in His Son, Jesus Christ***"

James 1:21-25 says,

*"…**RECEIVE** with meekness the **IMPLANTED
WORD**"*

How is the word **implanted?**

**The word; the gospel; the good news gets
implanted by the Spirit bearing strong
witness with our spirit, concerning the truth
of it,**

**It gets implanted by us believing it, by us
receiving and embracing it!**

21 *"…**RECEIVE** with meekness the
**IMPLANTED** WORD, **which IS ABLE to save
your souls**."*

In other words, it is able to SOZO *…***to SAVE,
to make whole and complete,** *"your soul*."

*…***and thus to rescue out of sin and
temptation to sin!**

22 *"BE DOERS; (BE BELIEVERS) OF THE
WORD and not just hearers, **ONLY
DECEIVING YOURSELVES STILL**"*

23 *"For if **anyone** is a hearer of THE WORD and not a doer (**a believer of it**),"*

*"...**HE IS LIKE A MAN <u>OBSERVING THE FACE OF HIS BIRTH</u>**,"*

(Note: Not his natural birth. No, he is observing **his true spirit origin, and the rebirth of his true spirit identity and design in Christ,**

...**he is observing it in the work of redemption!** — 1Peter 1:3,

...he is observing *that* birth, *that* face),

*"**<u>AS IN A MIRROR</u>**;"*

So, *"...**HE IS LIKE A MAN <u>OBSERVING THE FACE OF HIS BIRTH</u>**,* (...the face of his genesis; the face of his origin; *that* face; *that* birth,) **<u>AS IN A MIRROR</u>**;"*

*...when he hears the Word; when he hears the gospel; the* **good** <u>news</u> of **his** salvation **that took place in Christ, in the work of redemption!**

...and now James goes on to say:

24 *"**FOR HE OBSERVES HIMSELF** (his real design; his true identity; his true self; his new creation self),"*

*"BUT then goes away, and immediately forgets **WHAT KIND OF MAN <u>HE REALLY IS</u>**."*

232

25 *"But, he* (anyone) *who* **LOOKS INTO**
(gazes intently; truly beholds *and perceives
accurately;* with *faith;* with *persuasion*) **THE
PERFECT LAW; or THE LAW OF LIBERTY**
(THE LAW OF FAITH; or the *"word of TRUTH;"*
*that* **WORD that declares our perfect liberty**)

*…AND CONTINUES IN IT*

*"…***AND CONTINUES to believe it and totally
embracing it***"*

*"… and is not a forgetful hearer but a DOER
OF* **THE WORK***"*

**(In other words he is a believer who yields
to it and allows it to practically affect his life
and interaction with others),**

*"…***THIS ONE SHALL BE BLESSED IN WHAT
HE DOES***"*

**(He shall be blessed in his believing; by the
act of believing; literally blessed by FAITH.)**

There is a story written by Hans Christian
Anderson that has been retold over and over
again and has taken on many forms in different
cultures as it is told to children of different
ages.

The story might help bring further clarity to this
Scripture.

My version of it goes something like this:

On somebody's farm a swan's egg was placed under a mama duck.

As the little swan grew up with the rest of the ducks, *it became known as the ugly duckling,* because it never could quite fit in or feel completely at home living among the ducks, or even with being a duck, even though everybody, itself included, THOUGHT it was a duck.

Our little duckling at first tried to fit into duck society, *but because of its supposed inborn self-esteem problem or you can call it an inferiority complex if you wish,*

...but it was really *"an identity crises,"*

...so *because of* its identity crises, *it rebelled on purpose and began to act out its feelings of rejection, of not being accepted or quite being acceptable; it acted out its feeling that it didn't quite belong there among the ducks,* thus the name *'Ugly Duckling.'*

But in spite of all this, every time it saw some swans fly by, it was captivated by their grace and beauty *and was drawn to them by something inside of it that it couldn't explain.* It kept wishing that *it could be like them and be accepted by them,*

...but because it was convinced in its own little mind that it was but an ugly duckling, *it could never in its wildest dreams even contemplate the thought of receiving positive recognition from birds of the likes of them.*

You see, it thought to itself that there is no way that birds of the likes of swans *would ever accept a bird of the likes of it,*

*…in its mind, it was after all, an ugly duckling,* and nothing more.

To make a long story short, *after a long winter full of many trials and tribulations* our little ugly duckling grew up, and one day, **while swimming on the pond**, *it suddenly discovered to its amazement that it was indeed a most beautiful swan,*

*…**according to the reflection of its own face it was now intently looking at in the water.***

For a moment it couldn't believe its eyes, *but as it kept staring intently at that reflection, **the reflection of ITS OWN FACE**, right there in the water in front of it, as plain as anything,*

*…*suddenly the penny dropped, suddenly something inside of it clicked, *and **its faith came alive.***

*This new insight and understanding **set it completely free** from its whole identity crisis, and all its inferiority complexes, and it changed its whole life.*

It stopped ***trying to become*** a swan,

*…and it just began to live with the swans as a family member,*

***…for it was now, and really always had been, one of them.***

2Corinthians 5:17 & 18 says,

17 *"**THEREFORE, IF ANYONE** IS IN CHRIST JESUS…"*

The word *"IF"* in this Scripture **is a conclusion** and can also be translated as: *"**Since**"*

The *"THEREFORE"* is based on verse 14,

*"**If (or since) one died for all then all died**"*

…that is why this *"IF"* in verse 17 is still part of the same argument; of the same *conclusion* Paul came to in verse 14.

So this verse 17 can be read in this way:

*"**SINCE EVERYONE IS THEREFORE ALREADY in Christ**,"*

(Anyone, therefore, *who is* in Christ, *included in His death,* can *know* that…)

*"…**he is a new creation**,"*

*"**THEREFORE, IF ANYONE IS** IN CHRIST JESUS **he is a new creation** (he can also know that) **all the old things have passed***

236

*away, and that, **all things have become new**.”*

*“…**all the old things have passed away**…”*

*“…**all things have become new!**”*

I want you to note,

*“If one died **for all, THEN ALL DIED**” verse 14,*

*…**but we enter in through FAITH,** which is why this Scripture is written the way it is:*

2Corinthians 5:17, 18

17 *“Therefore, **if anyone** is in Christ Jesus,”*

Although everyone was in Christ, included in His death, just as Paul concluded in verse 14,

…yet he said: *“**if anyone,**” here in verse 17, **because we enter in through FAITH!**

**In other words, if you personally come to the conclusion Paul himself came to, *the conclusion of verse 14,***

*…***then it is only logical that that person should also come to the same conclusion of verse 17.***

**He will clearly see that,**

*“HE **IS** A NEW CREATION:*

**He will see and understand that,**

*"OLD THINGS **HAVE** PASS**ED** AWAY:"*

**He will,**

*"**BEHOLD** **ALL THINGS** **HAVE** BECOME NEW."*

18 *"**NOW** **ALL** THESE THINGS **ARE** OF GOD, who **has** RECONCILED **US** TO HIMSELF."*

Go back with me to James 1:18:

*"**OF HIS OWN WILL**,"*

(…of His own **desire,** by His own **LOGOS;**

…by revealing to us *that* WORD;

…**by revealing to us His own desire and His own design of us**),

*"HE BROUGHT US FORTH **BY THE WORD OF TRUTH**,"*

*"…**that we might be a kind of first fruits**,* (…and where there is first-fruits a harvest is sure to follow), ***of His creatures.***"

**It is only** *"THE WORD OF TRUTH"* **that is God's ability** *to preserve you blameless* **IN THE MIDST OF a crooked and perverse generation.**

**The tangible only comes** as a result of what you've heard!

Believe the word *and the tangible will follow!*

The truth *only reveals* how free you really are,

*…*and when you know it,

(*…*when you understand it, when you fully comprehend it, when you correctly perceive it, when you fully embrace it; when you believe it and become persuaded)

*…*then you shall be able to claim back your freedom *with ease* from the enemy,

*…*and you will be *able to walk* in that freedom!

Philippians 2:12 states,

*"THEREFORE my beloved brethren,* **WORK OUT** *(come to a logical, correct mathematical conclusion about) YOUR OWN SALVATION with fear and trembling…"*

Now why does he say: *"…with fear and trembling?"*

It is because *your enjoyment of salvation; your experience of it,* **depends on your correct conclusion.**

You cannot afford to come to any other conclusion about your salvation other than the correct one;

...than the one presented to you in *"the word of TRUTH"*

Philippians 2:12-13

12 *"**THEREFORE** my beloved brethren,* ***WORK OUT YOUR OWN SALVATION,*** **(Come to the correct conclusion for yourself)***"*

Why?

13 *"...**FOR** GOD **IS** AT WORK **IN** **YOU**,"*

How?

Through *"the word of TRUTH,"*

13 *"...**For** God **is** at work **in you, BOTH TO** **WILL**,* (In other words He is activating the desire in you) *...**AND TO DO**,* (He is also infusing you with zeal; with the anointing; with the power; with the ability, ***to live it out; to BE and to do***)

...**OF HIS GOOD PLEASURE**

(...to live out **in a practical way** what He has desired for you, and what He has designed you for, and declares you to be...)*"*

**Our personal conclusion about salvation *has everything to do with God's working inside us and through us.***

Philippians 2:14 says,

*"Do all things without murmuring and complaining or disputing…"*

(In other words; **don't resist God's working in you;** don't allow anything from the devil, any negative thing, *any questioning or unbelief or darkened understanding; any religious lie or self-deception or illusion or lust after sin* **to interrupt God's working in your heart.**)

Why?

What's God's purpose?

Philippians 2:15

*"…so that **YOU** may become **BLAMELESS AND INNOCENT,** CHILDREN OF GOD, **WITHOUT FAULT**…"*

*"…**IN THE MIDST OF** a crooked and perverse generation,"*

*"…**AMONG WHOM** YOU SHINE AS LIGHTS IN **THIS** WORLD…"*

**'How in the world do I get there; how do I become that, brother Rudi?'**

Philippians 2:16

*"…**<u>HOLDING FAST</u>** THE WORD OF LIFE…"*

***By fully <u>embracing</u> and <u>believing</u>** "THE WORD OF LIFE!"*

Can you see God's purpose, God's plan?

He has left us in this world *for our neighbor's sake,*

…for us to reveal God's knowledge to them *that they too might return to their Daddy and be made whole in His TRUTH and LOVE!*

If He just rescued us *for fellowship with Himself,*

…then God would have taken us home the minute we believed the *"word of TRUTH"* revealed in Jesus, and made that TRUTH Lord in our lives.

*There would be no reason for us to still be here then!*

Can you see why *"holding fast the word of life"* is so important?

The working of God within us and through us depends on it;

...the plan of God, YOUR VERY LIFE, YOUR SALVATION, *and also that of your neighbor,* depends on it.

1John 1:6 says

*"IF WE SAY we have fellowship with God, WHILE WALKING IN DARKNESS* (ignorance, confusion, lies, deception, half-truths)*, WE DECEIVE OURSELVES,"*

**(We end up living in sin, in other words, missing the mark; living outside of what we were designed for, because of it!)**

He says,

1John 1:6,

*"WE DECEIVE OURSELVES,* (in other words) *we lie* (if we keep saying then that we have fellowship with God) *and* (yet) *do not walk according to the truth."*

**You see; you cannot walk according to the truth unless you BELIEVE the TRUTH!**

So, correctly interpreted, he is saying that,

...because we *"do not (BELIEVE and THEREFORE) walk according to the truth,"*

...we end up walking in darkness: in confusion; and we give in to sin; *and we live a lie,* deceiving ourselves, *and we do not really have fellowship with God, because we don't really see eye to eye with Him in the truth;*

…we haven't embraced His TRUTH, *so how can we say we have embraced Him;*

…*we are not walking <u>in the same light</u> as Him;*

…we lie to ourselves, *or try to,* and we would like to *just pretend* that we do walk *in the same light* as Him, *even though deep down we know we don't.*

We lie to ourselves, because the alternative; the REALITY *is too difficult and unbearable to face and admit to.*

No one likes to admit to themselves or others for that matter *that they are living in a sort of hell of their own making.*

No one likes to admit to themselves or others that *they are on the way to a future hell because they have chosen darkness over light,*

…<u>and for all intents and purposes have rejected God and are living their life separate from God</u>;

…*because they are not agreeing with Him in the TRUTH!*

…*and not really seeing eye-to-eye with Him!*

**...even though *they may even pretend before others* that they do!**

Listen, *we do not have to walk in darkness and self-deception!*

We do not have to *live a lie* and live in *the bondage of our own idolatry to sin!*

There is no need *to pretend to have* fellowship with God

**...when REAL fellowship with God is available!**

*We don't have to live in bondage to lies and deception of our own making!*

We don't need to keep *living an empty life*;

*...we don't need to idolize and be in bondage to sin anymore*, trying to fill *the empty hole in our heart and life,* **when TRUTH and REAL FULFILMENT is available!**

*We can be **whole;** we can be **FREE INDEED!***

**We don't need to keep clinging to a false inferior identity,**

**...when our TRUE IDENTITY and our ORIGINAL AUTHENTIC DESIGN <u>has been revealed</u>!**

By FAITH in the TRUTH we can walk in INNOCENCE before God!

We can have REAL FRIENDSHIP AND FELLOWSHIP with God!

JESUS REDEEMED AND RESTORED AND DELIVERED US!

*We can choose to BELIEVE it and EMBRACE it!*

*We can choose to RETURN TO and EMBRACE our DADDY God and HIS LOVE FOR US!*

Galatians 1:4 is as clear as you can get!

It says that, JESUS,

*"...gave Himself up FOR OUR SINS, SO THAT HE MIGHT **DELIVER US** FROM **THIS PRESENT** EVIL AGE,"*

It was done, *"ACCORDING TO THE WILL OF GOD, **OUR FATHER**."*

In other words:

Our deliverance *"**FROM THIS PRESENT** EVIL AGE"* **was the will of God.**

God desired for us to be *"**DELIVERED**"* and *Jesus fulfilled His Father's desire.*

So, Jesus was doing *"**OUR FATHER'S**"* bidding when He *"**DELIVERED**"* us;

*…*and He delivered us,

*"**FROM THIS PRESENT** EVIL AGE"*

**He came and rescued us!**

**He came and redeemed and rescued our original design!**

**He came to restore that original image and likeness in us, *because we were designed for it!***

**He saw our un-fulfillment and our self-destruction, *living outside our design,***

*…***and He came *to restore us* and *to fulfill us* and *give our heart a home.***

**We belong in our Daddy's arms!**

**We belong there!**

**IN HIS LOVE!**

Verse 7 of 1John 1 says,

*"But IF WE **WALK** IN* (**believe and fully embrace**) ***THE LIGHT*** (The TRUTH), ***AS HE IS IN THE LIGHT***"

*"**AS HE IS IN THE LIGHT**"*

You see, this *"LIGHT;"*

...this insight; this understanding; this thought-process; this belief-system; this TRUTH; *this FAITH God is walking in,* AND WANTS US TO WALK IN,

...*IS HIS TESTIMONY OF US*!

It is His opinion;

It is *THE TRUTH about US,* (about the whole human race), *as revealed in Jesus Christ;* His WORD made flesh!

It is His FAITH;

*It is His understanding of the legal implications of His Son's suffering on OUR behalf!*

That is *the testimony of God!*

That is *the LIGHT He walks in*

...and wants us to walk in!

In closing, I urge you to get yourself a copy of *"The Mirror Bible"* available online at: www.friendsofthemirror.com or at www.amazon.com and several other book sellers.

If you want me or someone a part of our team to come to where you are, anywhere in the world, and give a talk or teach you and some of your friends about the gospel message, and redemption realities, simply contact us at www.livingwordintl.com ...or you can always find me on www.facebook.com

If you have been helped, or your perspective on life has changed, as a result of reading this book, please get in touch with me and let me know.

***I would love to share your joy,***

...so that my joy in writing this book may be full!

"When I consider Your heavens,
the works of Your fingers,
The moon and the stars,
which You have ordained,

What is man that You are
mindful
(that Your mind is full)
of him,

And the son of man that You
visit
(give attention to, or care for,
make so much of)
him?

For You have made him a little
lower than the angels
(than Elohim, God Himself);

And **You have crowned him with
glory and honor.**

**You have made him to have
dominion**
over the works of Your hands;

**You have put ALL things (in
subjection)
under his feet.**"
— Psalms 8:3-6

# About The Author

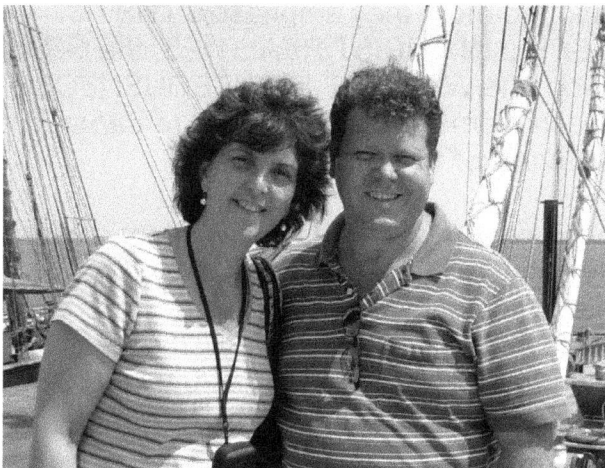

Rudi & Carmen Louw together oversee and pastor a church: Living Word International.

Rudi was born and raised in the country of South Africa while Carmen grew up in Cortland, New York. Today they travel and minister both locally and internationally.

They function in the ministry of reconciliation (2Corinthians 5:18-21) and flow strongly in the gifts of the Holy Spirit and His anointing to teach, preach, prophecy, heal *and whatever is needed to touch people's lives with the reality of God's love and power.*

God has given them keen insight into what He has to say to mankind in the work of redemption, *concerning the revelation of, and restoration of,* **humanity's true identity***,*

...and therefore they emphasize THE GOSPEL; IN CHRIST REALITIES; the GRACE of God; the WORD OF RIGHTEOUSNESS *and all such eternal truths* ***essential to salvation and living of the CHRIST-LIFE***

They have been granted this wisdom and revelation into the knowledge of God by the Spirit of Truth; by the resurrected Spirit of Jesus Christ Himself, *to establish and strengthen believers* ***in THE FAITH OF GOD, and to activate them in ministering to others.***

Not only are people set free from the poison and bondage of sin, condemnation and all kinds of intimidation, (upheld, strengthened and reinforced by age old religious ideas born out of ignorance and deception,) *but many are brought into a closer more intimate relationship with Father God,* ***as Daddy****, through accurate teaching, and unveiling of the gospel message, prophetic words, healings and miracles.*

Rudi & Carmen are closely knitted together with many other effective Christians, church fellowships, and groups of believers *who share the same revelation and passion* ***to impart God's TRUTH; to make disciples, and to impact the world with the LOVE OF GOD.***

www.ingramcontent.com/pod-product-compliance
Lightning Source LLC
Chambersburg PA
CBHW051818090426
42736CB00011B/1543